T0103694

時空的定義

一個台灣人，為大家所做的 2015 年物理總結。

The Definition of Spacetime
（with a Draft of English Translation）

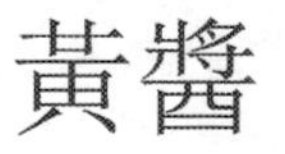

Order this book online at www.trafford.com
or email orders@trafford.com

Most Trafford titles are also available at major online book retailers.

Print information available on the last page.

ISBN: 978-1-4907-5842-8 (sc)
ISBN: 978-1-4907-5844-2 (hc)
ISBN: 978-1-4907-5843-5 (e)

Library of Congress Control Number: 2015905685

Trafford rev. 04/09/2015

www.trafford.com

North America & international
toll-free: 1 888 232 4444 (USA & Canada)
fax: 812 355 4082

給瓊英，伯彥和中彥

What I say & do today,
decide my future & define me.

今日的言行，造就明日的我。

目錄

序：兩小兒辯日

列子湯問篇，有一個很好的物理問題叫做“兩小兒辯日”。其原文如下：

孔子東游，見兩小兒辯鬥。問其故。一兒曰：「我以日始出時去人近，而日中時遠也。一兒以日初出遠，而日中時近也。」一兒曰：「日初出大如車蓋；及 日中，則如盤盂：此不為遠者小而近者大乎？」一兒曰：「日初出滄滄涼涼；及其日中如探湯：此不為近者熱而遠者涼乎？」子不 能決也。兩小兒笑曰：「孰為汝多知乎？」

列御寇是戰國時期的鄭國人，所以，那一個早在在西元前三百或四百年左右提出的問題，要一直等到人們明白陽光在大氣層的折射現象以後，人類才知道答案。

太陽在地平線下方的時候，光線因為折射而讓我們以為太陽在地平線上，而且，折射讓太陽的面積看起來比較大。工業化以後，空氣密度逐年增高，大氣層的折射率逐年增高，偏折就逐年變多，那麼，太陽在更低的地方就可以讓陽光折射到我們的眼睛。因此，除非人們控制了工業和運輸的廢氣排放量，否則，日出就會逐年提早，而日落會逐年延遲。

除了陽光折射的現象，還因為哥白尼（波蘭，1473-2-19 到 1543-5-24），伽利略（義大利，1564-2-15 到 1642-1-8）和牛頓（英國，1643-1-4 到 1727-3-31）等等科學家的努力，人們才不得不放棄托勒密（埃及，西元 90 年-168 年）的“天動理論”。

沖虛至德眞經卷第一

列子　張湛處度注

天瑞第一 夫巨細舛錯脩短殊性雖天地之大群品之衆涉於有生之分關於動用之域者存亡變化自然之符夫唯寂然至虛凝一而不變者非陰陽之所終始四時之所遷革

子列子 載子於姓上者首章或是弟子之所記故也 居鄭圃 鄭有圃田 四十年人无識者 非形不與物接言不與物交不知其德之至則同於不識者矣 國君卿大夫眎之猶衆庶也 非自隱於物直言无是非行无軌迹則物莫能知也 國不足 年饑 將嫁於衛 自家而出謂之嫁 弟子曰先生往无反期弟子敢有所謁先生將何以教先生不聞壺丘子林之言乎 壺丘子林列子之師 子列子笑曰壺子何言哉 四時行百物生豈假於言哉 雖然夫子嘗語伯昏瞀人吾側聞之試以告女 伯昏列子之友同學於壺子不言自受教於壺子者列子之謙者也 其言曰有生 今塊然之形也 不生 生物而不自生者也 有化 今存亡變改也 不化 化物而不自化者也 不生者能生生 不生者固生物之宗 不化者能化化 不化者固化物之主 生者不能不生化者不能不化 生者非能生而生化者非能化而化也直自不得不生不得不化者也 故常生常化 涉於有動之分者不得暫无也 常生常化者无時不生无時不化 生化相因存亡復往理无間也 陰陽爾四時爾 陰陽四時變化之物而復屬於有生之域者皆隨此陶運四時

所以列子在兩千三百年以前所提出的“兩小兒辯日”這個物理問題，也因此才有了完整的答案。就算“兩小兒辯日”是後人加到列子書上的故事，由東晉張湛給它注解也是將近一千六百年以前的事了。所以，好問題，往往不容易解答。

然而，就算當初有人對那個物理問題深入追究下去，千年之內，卻有誰能夠知道“大氣層”這種東西？又有誰想像得出大地是球狀的，而且地球除了繞太陽公轉還在自傳？所以，一個好問題不一定能夠很快找到答案。但是人類知識的累積，靠的就是好問題和它的好答案。

現在，人們還有很多問題沒有答案。比較貼身的問題例如麥田圈是怎麼雕出來的？有沒有不明飛行物？有沒有鬼？有沒有神？為什麼沒有天然的反粒子？為什麼光子的速度不受發光體速度的影響？乃至於，引力是不是因為異電荷的吸力稍微大於同電荷的斥力所造成的？這些都是年輕人的囊中物。

但是，像“兩小兒辯日”這樣的好問題，可遇而不可求；因為，它問的是“一個人們必須解開的矛盾”。

像抽水馬桶，下水道和污水處理系統，電，電報，電話，電燈，電影，無線電，電冰箱，電視，電腦，電腦網路，智慧手機等等也都是精彩的好問題所帶動的發明。可是，這一類精彩的好問題大多是“如何做”的問題，也許有一些“為什麼”的問題，但是它們不是“必須解開的矛盾”。

人類最近的“一個人們必須解開的矛盾”是在 1881 年，由邁克生（美國，1852-12-19 到 1931-5-9）所構想的一個觀測乙太的實驗。

這本書就從這一個人們必須解開而尚未解開的矛盾出發，去定義時間和空間。然後再提出另外兩個人們必須解開的矛盾，和讀者共同研究。

最後我提出一個我最近想到的，可能解開矛盾的辦法。

這是拋磚引玉，希望讀者們一起用心來解開矛盾。

黃醬
2015 年 3 月 15 日

時空的定義

一個台灣人，為大家所做的
2015 年物理總結。

1. 未解開的矛盾

因為 1881 年那個實驗太粗糙，所以邁克生先生在 1887 年和莫立（美國，1838-1-29 到 1923-2-24）合作進行了出名的邁克生-莫立實驗（Michelson-Morley Experiment，MMX）。

人們在不同地點、不同時間多次重複了邁克生－莫立實驗，精密度不斷提高。綜合相關實驗結果，多數科學家們的解釋是，地球不存在相對以太的運動；所以，他們必須接受洛倫茲轉換（洛轉）來解決這個矛盾。

經過上個世紀一百年的民主潮流冲擊，洛轉終於在多數科學家的擁戴下，坐穩了它在物理教科書上的地位。

多數科學家都接受了“動尺缩收”和“動鐘遲緩”這兩個假說，從而把二十世紀以前的時間和空間概念給徹底改變了。

但是，科學家們對於“MMX”這個必須解開的矛盾所做的解釋並不像他們對“兩小兒辯日”所解釋的那樣清清楚楚。

1-1. 未解開的實驗矛盾

科學家們對“MMX”的解釋至少有兩點不清楚。第一個不清楚的地方是，科學家們隱藏了一個秘密：Ives-Stilwell 實驗的結果和狹義相對論（狹相）預估的結果，在“平均波長的變動方向上”完全相反。但是科學家們只強調“波長變動誤差”的成果，不提“方向”不合。詳情請看本書 3-1 節。

1-2. 未解開的數學矛盾

另外一個沒有解釋清楚的地方是，洛轉在數學上的證明。愛因斯坦分別在 1905 年和 1920 年證明了兩次洛轉，但是都失敗了。您可以參考 “Special Relativity of Roses & Happiness” 書上的說明。其他人的證明也不完整。

1-3. 很容易解開的矛盾

“MMX” 這個必須解開的矛盾，其實很容易解決。只要把光子的速度和光源的速度關係徹底弄明白，MMX 就沒有矛盾了。您可以參考 “Lorentz Transformation for High School Students” 書上的說明。

可是，多數物理學家們既不用數學的向量去分析光子的速度和光源的速度關係；也不去檢驗洛轉的多種數學證明究竟錯在哪些步驟。他們硬是用洛轉，狹相和廣相去解開 MMX 那個矛盾。

1-4. 20 世紀的偽科學

其實洛轉，狹相和廣相是 20 世紀的偽科學。

首先，在名字上，狹相和廣相已經是假的。當狹相在 1905 年 6 月 30 日的論文把它的應用範圍從洛轉的相對等速度擴充到相對等速率，那個動作就已經把狹相的“逆狹相”給拿掉了。人們可以假設“逆洛轉”，但是，在 GPS 的情況，等速率圓周運動是不存在“逆狹相”的。所以，擴充以後的狹相，其實已經失去“古典相對論”的資格。

在現實裡頭，顯然沒有“逆廣相”而理論上“重力強度”也沒有“逆重力強度”這個東西。所以，狹相和廣相必須把時空混淆，離開古典的相對論，在四維時空裡頭，去玩固定原點的旋轉把戲。

其次，在定義上，逆洛轉和狹相無法並存。當動系的觀測員用缩收的動尺和遲緩的動鐘去測量靜系的相對速度時，靜系的速度是 v 的 γ 平方倍。所以加上狹相，逆洛轉就無法存在了。

另外，在數學上，狹相無法滿足函數運算：如果 S’’相對於 S’做等速度 v 運動，我們用 γ=f(v)來表達 γ 和速度 v 的關係，那麼，根據狹相公式，t’’ = t / f(2v)；可是，t’’= t’/f(v) 而 t’=t/f(v) 所以 t’’ = t / ((f(v))^2)。然而 f(2v)=(f(v))^2 卻只有在 v=0 或 v > c 時才成立。

而且，在邏輯上，假設 S 是宇宙靜系，那麼，如果觀測員 O 和 O’ 把尺沿著 x 軸放著；根據洛轉，觀測員 O 的尺就比觀測員 O’ 的尺長一些。可是，如果我們讓逆洛轉也成立的話，反之亦然，而兩把真實的尺卻不可能互相比對方更長。

所以不論在名字上，定義上，數學上或者邏輯上來說它們都是一組偽科學。

1-5. 尚未解開的矛盾

我將在第三章詳細說明，為什麼 MMX 對多數物理學家來說，仍然是一個尚未解開的矛盾。

在“時空的定義”這本書裡頭，我要介紹一個可以取代洛轉的方程組，叫做“距離轉換”（距轉）。

如果伽利略轉換（伽轉）是一個理論版本，那麼，距轉就是一個伽轉的實用版本。

另外，我要推薦湯克雲的“動態引力公式”。如果牛頓的引力公式只適合靜止的兩個星球，那麼，湯克雲的“動態引力公式”就可以用在移動的兩個星球之間。

實用版的伽轉以及動態的引力公式，在絕對時空裡頭，完全可以應付科技上的各種需求。

在靜止的 **絕對空間** 裡頭，以固定速度前進的 **絕對時間** 把一個個連續的 **事件** 推向 **歷史**。

在這樣一個簡單明白的朗朗時空，中國文化主張全心“入世”，追求“大同世界”。在這一類文化裡面的人，他們不知道靈魂可以存活多久，也許 7 天，也許 49 天，然後消逝；但是，他們又希望祖先和歷史義人的靈魂能夠永遠在天上保祐他們。

印度和佛教文化主張“輪迴”，追求靈魂“出世”。希望靈魂可以脫離困苦的現世，進入西方極樂世界，不再輪迴。

天主，基督和回教文化主張“信神”，追求靈魂“出世”。希望在死後，靈魂可以與神同住天堂，不再回到現世。

雖然大家主張和追求的不太一樣，然而“尋真，行善，求義”這個生活指導方針，卻是人類多種文化的共識。

在尋真的路上，我要給時間和空間做一個完美的定義，再提出兩個“人們必須解開的矛盾”。且讓我先來介紹被 20 世紀扭曲的現代時空。

2. 民主與科學

多數人的意見很簡單，只有兩點：

有利和可行。

於是，當愛因斯坦在 1905 年 6 月 30 日的論文中，宣稱他已經在數學上證明了“洛倫茲轉換”（洛轉）；二十世紀的科學就此走向了民主之路。

為什麼呢？

2-1. 民主科學 - 天時和地利

我們先研究“天時和地利”這兩個因素。

當時歐洲多數的物理學家正在懷疑那個拖延十多年的“動尺缩收”假說能否解決當時最嚴重的科學問題。那個問題是當時的科學家們大多認為：MMX 證誤了“乙太”理論。

如果他們突然聽到有人在數學上證明了“動尺缩收”假說，那麼，您認為他們能夠找到的，最有利的，可行之道是什麼呢？

我想，多數人的選擇是“我的團隊要趕快設計實驗去證明它”。

2-2. 民主科學 - 事件本身

接下來在“事件”的因素上，當然也有學者懷疑愛因斯坦的證明是否嚴密。

但是在物理學界，實驗結果往往比數學證明更加重要；何況，愛因斯坦還在同一篇論文中提出了一個令人驚艷的新假說。那就是主張“動鐘遲緩”的狹義相對論（狹相）。

所以，在洛轉的“動尺缩收”事件上，科學家不但研究物質壓缩的可能性，多數物理學家還開始積極研究愛因斯坦的狹相理論，看看時間是不是能夠被狹相的公式，成功的減速。

2-3. 民主科學 -人和因素

在“人和”的因素上，到了 1907 年，愛因斯坦的老師已經幫他把 Poincare 的第四維坐標“ict”概念，建立成“閔氏時空”，讓愛因斯坦的狹義相對論能夠擁有幾何上的意義。

在同一年，愛因斯坦開始思考廣義相對論（廣相）並且在 1915 年完成草案。

在 1916 年愛因斯坦正式發表廣相以後才一個月，Karl Schwazschild 就提出廣相“場方程式”的第一個非簡解答。人多好辦事，很快的，黑洞理論就成為廣相的第一個大成就。

雖然在 1917 年愛因斯坦給自己的廣相加上一個宇宙常數，但是，在 1929 年提出的宇宙擴張理論還是讓愛因斯坦保住了 1915 年的原版廣相。

2-4. 民主科學 - 物力因素

在“物力”的因素上，由於原子，核子，粒子 以及電腦和網路的迅速發展，也不知道是幸或不幸，始作俑者的洛轉以及愛因斯坦的狹相和廣相就經由多數物理科學家的推選，進入了“知識”的殿堂。

於是，過了 1960 年到 1975 那個“廣相的黃金時期”以後，即使廣相理論和量子理論無法共存，就算沒有實驗證明“動尺缩收”假說；當今多數物理科學家仍然決定把那兩個科技無法證明的“動尺缩收”和“動鐘遲緩”假說，當作是已經證明的物理事實。

在這些有利的因素下，二十世紀的科學就此走向了時空錯亂的民主之路。

2-5. 科學

科學和民主各有兩個重點，科學的重點比較簡單：

合實和合理。

而且，在真相不明的情況下，科學便只剩下一個重點，也就是合理。那麼“動尺缩收”和“動鐘遲緩”這兩個假設的物理現象是否合理呢？

且讓我先在這一章簡單說明“邏輯”和“物理”，這兩個相關的名詞，以及“生命力”和“搶先”這兩個現象，然後再從實際的科學事件中，挑選兩個事實來說明“動尺缩收”和“動鐘遲緩”這兩個假設的物理現象，既不合事實也不合邏輯，所以不合理。

2-6. 邏輯

數學是學習邏輯的最佳教材。所謂合理，就是在邏輯上合乎事實。所以邏輯是檢驗合不合理的工具。

所謂邏輯就是在做選擇的時候，找出最關鍵的“一個因素”。

但是，邏輯卻不是一般人喜歡使用的工具。

多數人很少使用邏輯去辦事。對超過半數的人來說， 他們所面對的選擇往往是“被動的”；您也知道，一般而言，在被迫去做選擇的時候，都只剩下一些不得已的少數選項。

中國有俗話說，聖者先機而動，賢者見機而變，凡者順機而行，愚者失機而悔；既然聖賢者總居少數，那麼，民主的“選擇”就大多是順機而行或失機而悔的。

所謂順機而行，是隨著賢者的變動，有樣學樣；卻已經慢了半拍。慢半拍，就是在少數選項中，去找一個壞處比較少的選項；那麼，後悔的機會就比較大，是不是？

選首長有可能如是，選法律條款大多如是；我認為，投票選擇科學知識呢，就只能如是。

2-7. 物理

數學這個邏輯教材和物理這門科學有兩個無法接軌的地方：極大和極小。

在極大方面，物理物件的數目總是有限而數字可以無限多。在極小方面，物理物件總有非零的質能而數學的點，線和面沒有體積也沒有質能。

可是，所謂科學偏偏是包含“公式”的知識。科學必須包含公式而公式裡頭的數字就把物理連上了數學。

2-8. 生命力

物理這門學問在面對“合實”檢定的時候，還有一個致命傷，那就是“生命力”。

生命力讓一個活體可以反物理而動。物理學家完全無法知道在什麼時刻，什麼地方，以及何種情況下，一個活體會進行什麼樣的反物理動作。

更何況一個正在從事科學研究的人，一個科學家，也是一個活體。那個活體不但可以反物理而動，在失控時，還可能逆常情而動。

2-9. 搶先

所以，像洛轉這種在數學上完全忽略函數定理而且還不能充分實證的科學結論，到了多數平庸的物理學家手中，就硬是變成了“奇貨可居”。建立在洛轉上面的狹相和廣相也就跟著“熱門”起來。

那就好像在未做好地質探勘的地面，為了搶商機，趕著動工構築百層高樓。

您想想看，既然看起來廣相好像“快要”被證明了，而廣相建立在狹相上，狹相建立在洛轉上，洛轉又好像已經被愛因斯坦和其他學者用數學證明了，那麼，學校和政府也只能夠理所當然的“搶著”把錢花在廣相和狹相的研究上，是不是？

大家都希望“自己的機構”在科學基礎的發展上，能夠“領先”全球，對不對？

3. 假設的時空現象

現在，先讓我用兩個證據來簡單說明為什麼二十世紀的科學“已經”走入了時空錯亂的民主化科學之路。

首先讓我們想想科學的基礎。由於生物的心靈既無法詳細的觀測也無法明白的記錄下來，所以心靈完全超乎科學的處理能力。也所以科學能夠處理的最大範圍就是物理，包括生物的身體，或者說，生物的物質部分。

那麼，物理的基礎是什麼呢？既然物理是一門科學，科學離不開記錄，記錄又離不開事件時刻和地點；所以不管記錄的是什麼事件，都必須記下事件的時空。

分析到此，我們可以說，明確的時空觀念就是物理和科學的基礎。

恰巧，二十世紀的科學新理論裡頭，除了測不準原理，最勁爆的就是“動尺縮收”和“動鐘遲緩”這兩個假設的時空現象。

那兩個假說，分別提出了兩個和時空相關的公式，而“時空”這個物理基礎也終於在 20 世紀，被那兩個公式，給完全顛覆了。

洛轉的“動尺縮收方程組”和狹相的“動鐘遲緩公式”對今天的知識分子而言，已經是收入教科書裡頭，教給學生們的物理知識。

但是，在“動鐘遲緩”的狹相實驗裡頭，投贊成票的物理科學家們偷偷的藏起了一個刻意隱瞞的事實。而且在代表“動尺縮收”的洛轉裡頭，經過仔細檢查，在數學上，它的時間公式居然是“動鐘加速”！讓我分別說明如下。

3-1. Ives-Stilwell 實驗（1938）

那個實驗的結果，和狹相的預期結果方向相反。狹相預期光源與觀測者的相對速度越大，測得的波長平均值就比靜止的波長值大得越多。

可是實驗的結果是，相對速度越大測得的波長平均值就比靜止的波長值小得越多。

於是多數物理科學家們共同決定，只考慮 Doppler 效應和實驗結果的“差額”，不考慮測得的波長數值是變大或變小。反正 Doppler 效應預期不變，而實驗結果，速度越快，“差額”變得越大，那已經證明了 Doppler 效應必須被修改。

少數物理學家提出一些質疑，但是，多數物理學家主張“該實驗的結果支持狹相”；於是這個明顯的“狹相證誤”就被民主票選給轉變成“狹相證明”了。

3-2. 洛轉的真相 （1889/1892）

根據“Lorentz Transformation for High School Students”那一本書，洛轉的正確數學結論可以分兩種情況來表達。

在兩個系統相對速度為零的時候，$\gamma = 1$，所以 (t’, x’, y’, z’) = (t, x, y, z)；這個在邏輯上和洛轉吻合。但是，而在相對速度大於零的時候，洛轉公式可以被證明是

$$(t', x', y', z') = (\gamma t, -\gamma vt, y, z)$$。

也就是說，有人用邏輯證明了在 $v > 0$ 的情況，洛轉的時間方程式必須是 $t' = \gamma t$。所以在數學上，洛轉主張的其實是“動鐘加速”，正好和狹相相反。

可是該書的作者默默無名，洛轉的以上真相自然而然就被“票選”這個事實給掩蓋了。換句話說，事實上，該書的邏輯論證根本不可能被教科書提名，當然也就不可能被票選進入教科書裡頭了。

4. 時空的真相

廣相主張“壓鐘遲緩”，力場越強，時間越慢。

愛因斯坦還把古典物理的空間和時間用力場結合為四維時空；力場包括重力，動力和動力以外的各種非重力，而且，愛因斯坦把“動力以外的各種非重力”和“重力”用“等價原理”來簡化。那麼物體就會尋找彎曲時空裡頭的最短路線去移動。

廣相主張，時空告訴物質如何移動，而物質告訴時空如何彎曲。

現代的知識分子已經相信，愛因斯坦的廣相，在極弱力場裡頭就簡化為狹相；而狹相在相對速度極慢時就簡化為古典的牛頓物理。

在這一章，我將針對“動尺縮收”，“動鐘遲緩”和“壓鐘遲緩”來仔細說明時空的真相。

4-1. 動尺缩收

在事實上，就算“動尺缩收”真的發生了；動系觀測員所測量到的事件位置坐標值和靜系觀測員所測量到的事件位置坐標值，並不像洛轉的空間公式所描述的那麼簡單。

首先，伽利略轉換（伽轉）空間公式的原始形式，在數學上，其實是 x’ = x-vt’。只因為在伽轉裡頭 t’ = t 永遠成立，所以 x’ = x-vt 也就跟著成立。可是洛轉裡頭的 t’和 t 不一定相同，洛轉應該用伽轉的原始空間公式去添加“動尺缩收”這個假說，那樣才是正確的做法。

其次，究竟事件發生在動系或靜系裡頭?

如果先後兩個事件都發生在動系裡頭，好比都發生在火車上，那麼，兩個事件的空間距離就隨著火車上標記事件地點的物件，好比車上的鋼柱位置或廣告位置，而跟動尺做同樣的收缩，所以測量出來的距離不因火車的速度而變；除非觀測員知道自己在動, 把事件地點標示在地面的物件上，然後用“動尺”去量兩個標示點的距離。

所以，兩個事件都發生在動系的結果多半和“動尺缩收”的那個“動”的假設不合。反而，靜止的觀測員會認為“前事件”的“車上那個地點”，在測量“後事件”的時候，已經移動了 v(t2-t1) 的距離。

如果先後兩個事件都發生在靜系裡頭，那就吻合“動尺缩收”的情況。當然，如果一個事件發生在靜系，另一個事件發生在動系，測量的工作就更加複雜。

對於以上兩個因素，物理學者們並沒有一個共識。

愛因斯坦還讓所有事件都發生在動系裡頭的一個非常特別的範圍裡頭。那個範圍是，包含動系原點而垂直於 x’軸的平面上，所以 x’=0。然後愛因斯坦在那一個條件下，混淆了“動尺缩收”的“動”字前提，去推論出他的狹相公式。

發生在那個平面上的任何兩個事件的距離，根本不受“動尺缩收”這個條件影響；因為，根據洛轉的方程組，y’=y，z’=z 而在那個平面上，x’=0；所以，對於動系的觀測員來說，不論相對速度 v 有多快，事件距離的測量完全不受“動尺缩收”的影響。

對於“動”和“靜”的共識實在需要物理學者們三思，然後給人們一個明明白白的解釋。

4-2. 三度空間裡頭的怪物

接著我們看看在“動尺缩收”的世界裡頭，我們都變成什麼樣的怪物。

如果太空船的速度大於光速的 0.867 倍，也就是如果 $v > 0.867c$，那麼動尺在移動方向的收缩程度就大於 50%。

換句話說，太空船的駕駛員如果轉頭和副駕駛員說話，他的頭就從大餅臉變成馬臉；他回過頭，看著太空船的前進方向，又回到大餅臉。您認為我們的頭骨有辦法應付這種快速轉變嗎？

4-3. 動鐘遲緩和壓鐘遲緩

愛因斯坦在 1905 年介紹狹相的時候，就讓狹相公式脫離洛轉的限制。他讓“動鐘遲緩”的應用範圍，包括速率相同而方向不同的圓周運動。於是才有了所謂的“GPS 的應用”。

但是，他沒有進一步去了解時鐘和時間的關係。他沒有去思考，在時鐘速度改變的情況下，時間的速度會不會受到任何影響？

他的相對論論文，沒有給出完整的“時間”定義。物理學家們對於“時間”這個名詞，也還沒有共同的定義。

但是，在今天的物理學裡頭，物理學家們卻已經用最接近相對論公式的原子鐘去代表光陰的速度。GPS 定位系統也就因此被物理學家們拿來證明狹相和廣相是對的。

對物理學家來說，違反廣相理論的“鐘擺鐘”就不能代表光陰的速度。因為它是“壓鐘加速”。

如果有未來的時鐘能夠不受地心引力的影響，那麼，對於今日的多數物理學家來說，那種不受地心引力影響的未來時鐘，也不能代表光陰的速度。

對於今日的多數物理學家來說，只有吻合廣相“壓鐘遲緩”公式的時鐘才能夠準確標示“當地”的光陰速度。

廣相規定，符合“壓鐘遲緩”公式的時鐘才是標準鐘。您說，如果廣相需要依靠這種方法去支持它的成立；那麼，科學不是太兒戲了嗎？

4-4. 兩個觀測員的洛轉

洛轉和伽轉的最大差別是洛轉指定了觀測員而伽轉則安排了無限多的觀測員。他們的觀測員對於事件時刻的測量結果也就不一樣。

一般教科書讓洛轉的觀測員 O 和 O’分別坐在靜系 S 和動系 S’ 的原點。您知道，如果“一個事件地點”離 O 比較近而離 O’ 比較遠，O 就比較早觀測到那個事件。

可是，如果在 S 和 S’ 裡頭每個地方都有觀測員，那麼 O 和 O’ 就可以讓位於那個事件地點的觀測員去記錄事件時刻，從而得到相同的事件時刻；那就是伽轉裡頭的公式， t’ = t。

這是一個明明白白的事實，所以，我們就從這個事實出發去定義“時間”。

4-5. 一個事件時刻

要了解兩個觀測員記錄的時間速度到底有什麼不同，我們需要對“一個事件時刻”有簡單明白的觀念。

也許您看過“來自星星的你”那部韓劇，在花轎衝出懸崖的那一刻，男主角把時間給凝固了。

花轎衝出懸崖

三個時刻的冷凍宇宙
兩個時間

在真實世界，時間是不能夠停留的。世界歷史也就由一個接一個，連續的，冷凍宇宙給表達出來。換句話說，那些一個接一個，連續的，事件時刻也就合成了“光陰”。現代人把“光陰”也叫做“時間”。就字面上，我們可以說

兩個“事件時刻”之間，就是“時間”。

那麼，光陰就包括了時刻和時間。在需要區別意義的時候，兩個“事件時刻”之間的“光陰”可以用“時段”來稱呼。所以，時間（光陰）包括時刻和時段。

在任意兩個不同的事件時刻之間，總有無限多的事件時刻把那一個時段填滿。

在數字裡頭，“圓周率”和“2 的平方根”都是人們熟知的無理數，所以分數（有理數）是一個不連續的數字系統。

包含有理數和無理數的實數則是最小的連續數字系統。所以在數學上，我們可以把“一個事件時刻”對應到“光陰實數軸”上面的一個點，那樣，兩個“事件時刻點”之間，就有無限多個連續的“事件時刻點”。

在這樣安排的時軸裡頭，數學的“無限小”概念和物理的“連續光陰”這個“時間”事實就可以完全吻合。

時間（或者更明確的說，光陰）不是一個物理物件，它是兩大物理基礎之一。另一個物理基礎，空間，也不是一個物理物件。

時間和空間互相獨立，它們又獨立於物理物件之外；

但是，

在每一個物理事件和每一個生理事件中，它們都是“事件記錄”的必要項目。

4-6. 時軸

如果我們選定光陰實數軸上的一個點來代表“現在”這個事件，那麼，過去的每一個事件都恰好可以在光陰實數軸，代表過去的射線上，找到唯一的事件時刻點來對應那一個事件。

在一個事件時刻的冷凍宇宙裡頭，其實有許多的事件給凝固在一起。那些事件的事件時刻當然相同。然而，明明具有相同事件時刻的兩個事件，在不同的觀測員記錄中，卻往往有不同的時刻數值。

造成這種結果有兩個主要因素：一個是在科技上，他們的時鐘無法百分百同步；另一個是他們和事件地點的距離往往不同。

我在 4-5 那一節把光陰實數軸叫做“時軸”。

4-7. 兩個想像事件時刻

現在我要用兩個“想像”事件來說明時軸上的“事件時刻”為什麼獨立於“時鐘的速度”。也就是說，為什麼光陰的速度只有一個？然後您就明白，“光陰的速度”其實就是“光速”，而一個不受環境影響的計時器才是最理想的計時器。

假設洛轉裡頭，在地球上相互以等速度 v 移動的兩個觀測員 O 和 O’ 附近，有一個位於路邊 A 點的燈泡。

事件 E1 是燈泡在時刻 t1 開，
事件 E2 是燈泡在時刻 t2 關。

那麼，在 t1 時刻的冷凍宇宙裡頭，O，O’ 和 A 三點標示在地球上的位置與 t2 時刻的冷凍宇宙裡頭 O，O’和 A 這三個點在地球上的位置，只有 A 是必定相同的；因為，O 和 O’都可能在地球上移動，好比 O 的速度是 v 而 O’的速度是 2v。

然而，因為地球不停的自轉，所以在宇宙中，A 的兩次位置反而必定不同。

我們假設在 t1 時刻的冷凍宇宙裡頭，三點分別為 O1， O'1 和 A1；而在 t2 時刻的冷凍宇宙裡頭，分別為 O2，O'2 和 A2。現在就讓我們來研究一下，這兩個“事件時刻”之間的那一段“時間”。

4-8. 一個絕對靜止點

如果想像我們也看得到沒有進入瞳孔的光子，那麼，我們就可以看見兩個光球球皮所包住的一層光殼。

它的厚度大約是 (t2-t1)c。

外皮的球心是 A1 點而內皮的球心是 A2 點。

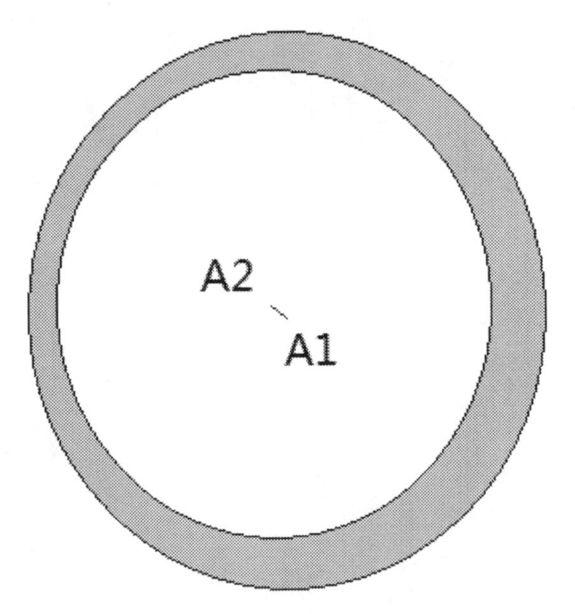

這一層光殼，以光速連續擴大，但是，
光殼裡頭所包含的光子數量不變，所以
它的光子密度與半徑平方成反比（因為，
光殼厚度固定）。所以，這個光殼越走
越淡。

理論上，在時刻 t1 的那個冷凍宇宙，A1 點就像是“宇宙爆炸論”的起爆點；所有外皮上的光子全部都集中在那一個 A1 點。

當 A 點在宇宙中由 A1 走到 A2 的時候，外皮的半徑大約是 (t2-t1)c，而 A2 正是內皮球心的位置。

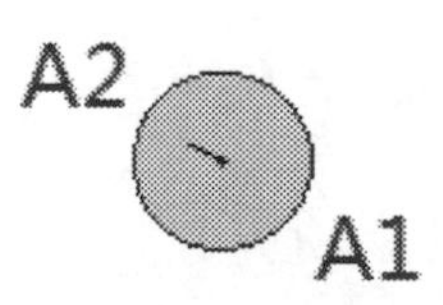

在 t2 時刻，點A2聚集了
所有內皮上的光子。

在時刻 t2 以後，這個球殼最薄的地方大約就在，由 A1 指向 A2，然後碰到外球殼的位置；反過來，和那個位置與球心 A1 對稱的點，球殼最厚。

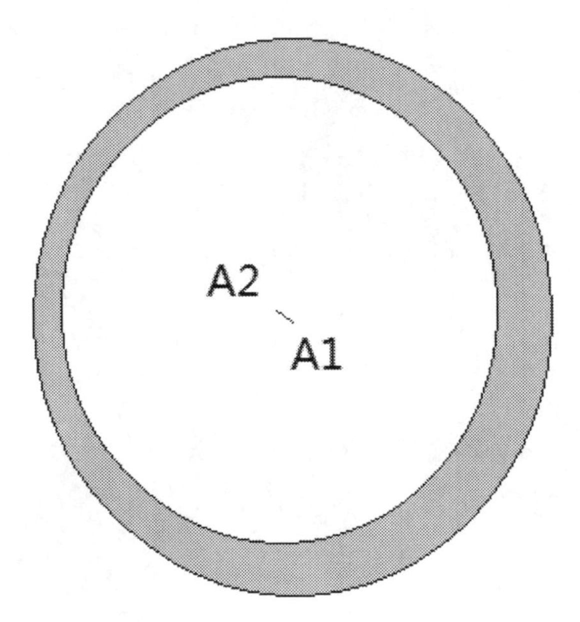

光殼的外皮什麼時刻碰到地球上的觀測員 O 和 O’，O 和 O’就各自記錄下事件 E1 的事件時刻 t1o 和 t1o’。

同樣的，光殼的內皮到達觀測員的時刻，事件 E2 就分別被記錄下事件時刻 t2o 和 t2o’。

如果因為(t2o-t1o)和(t2o’-t1o’)不同就說 O 和 O’的光陰速度不同，那麼，已經明白時間定義的您就可以很清楚的說，那是一個錯誤的認知。

那個差異，乃是兩個同一型號的“計時器”距離事件地點不同或者受到環境影響（例如重力和溫度不同），所造成的結果。事實上，在兩個冷凍宇宙之間，O 和 O’經歷了相同長度的光陰。

如果 t2 和 t1 非常接近，那麼，光殼就非常薄。最薄的情況是只有外皮，也就是 t2=t1。

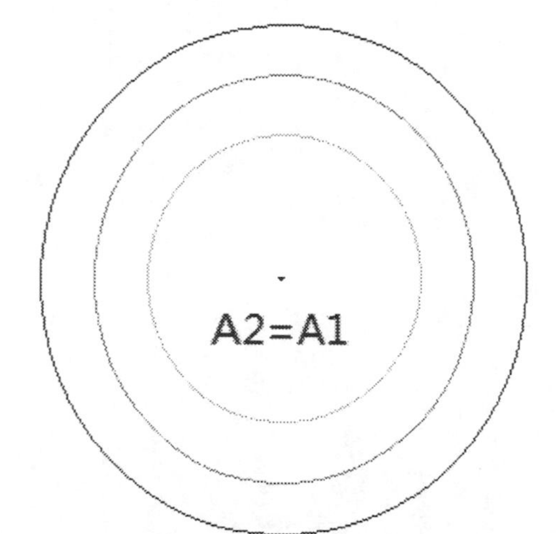

當t2=t1時，A2=A1，只有一層逐漸擴大的光皮。

如果 t2=t1，那麼，A2=A1 那一個點就是一個，宇宙裡頭的絕對靜止點。

如果在正方體的一個頂點和與它相鄰的三個頂點各放一個燈泡，同時開關，那麼，在理論上，如果 t2=t1 人們就有四個絕對靜止點可以給絕對靜止空間設立一個直角坐標系。

4-9. 絕對光陰速度

事實上，在 t2 和 t1 的兩個冷凍宇宙之間，O 和 O’經歷了相同長度的光陰。即使 O 在山腳而 O’在山頂，他們所度量的兩個事件“時段”也許有些差異，但是，您已經很清楚，在兩個冷凍宇宙之間，O 和 O’應該經歷相同的“時間”。那麼，究竟那個相同的“時間”應該，或者可以，如何度量呢？光陰的速度應該怎麼去了解呢？

在宇宙中，每一個光子，在兩個冷凍宇宙之間，所移動的路線長度都一樣，(t2-t1)c。

在介質裡頭，光子走過的路線是鋸齒狀的；雖然，測量出來的速度較慢，但是，速率是一樣的。

在山上測量或在山下測量，光速相同。

那麼，我們為什麼不用那個一致的路線長度去度量光陰的速度？如果我們同意，

那麼光陰的速度就是光速。

把現在人類的計時單位“秒”用原子鐘來度量，光速大約是每秒三億公尺。“一寸光陰一寸金”而秒是“禾少“，如果我們建立一個新字，把“禾”與“寸”併成一個字“禾寸”，那麼我們可以規定光子的速度是每一個“禾寸”走一公尺；那麼，一個“禾寸”就大約是三億分之一秒。

當然，如果人們以光速和秒來定義“公尺”這個“長度”，那麼，人們就必須先依賴那個“會因環境而變的計時器”去讀“秒”然後找到長度。

所以，我想用波長來定義“公尺”，那樣做，1 公尺大約是 1877934 個綠光的平均波長（大約 1877934 x 532.5 奈米）。

所以，用越高頻率的波長來定義 1 公尺，就越精密。一個“禾寸”就是光子走過大約 1877934 個綠光平均波長，大約 1877934 x 532.5 奈米，那個長度所花費的時段。

因為光速不變，綠光的平均波長也不變，所以“禾寸”不變。

我們自然可以數綠光的波數來計時。在一個“綠光錶”裡頭，把綠光光束射向接收器，每數完 1877934 個波峰，就增加一個“禾寸”。

希望在山頂和山腳，赤道和北極，綠光不會改變它的波長，那麼，在地球上我們就有了“絕對鐘錶”。

這個新的光陰單位“禾寸”就讀做“寸”。英語翻譯是 photond，簡寫成 pho。

一個 second 大約是 299792458 個 photond，也就是 1 sec = 299792458 pho。

光速就是：1 meter/photond。

如果我們採用更高頻率的光束來當“光錶”當然可以把“光陰”標示的更加精密；但是，知足常樂，如果真的有“綠光錶”可以用，人類就應該偷笑了。

5. 蔡志忠

蔡先生在 2010 年的“東方宇宙三部曲”裡頭主張

“相對於一個光源，受光體的時間 t 永遠等於（觀測的總波數 X 波長）/光速”。

他提到，如果我們以光速離開光源，那不是沒有光波會通過我們嗎？那麼，要如何計算時間呢？

他的答案是，永遠也不會有這種情形發生，因為非零質點的速度一定小於光速。

他說，這也可能是“自然”大發慈悲，菩薩心腸的一面。

5-1. 孿生子悖論

蔡先生以美國職籃（NBA）決賽轉播為例說明如何利用他的時間公式去了解孿生子悖論。在決賽開打時，雙生子哥哥以 0.8 光速到 0.8 光時遠的地方再回到地球，一路觀看轉播，兩小時後球賽結束而哥哥也回到地球。

按照狹相，哥哥在旅程所花的時間因為“動鐘遲緩”只經過 1.2 小時，而弟弟經歷了 2 小時。

現在，我們用蔡先生的時間公式去檢查這個決賽轉播。

去程，因為哥哥以 0.8 光速離開，所以轉播的電磁波（不可見光波）只有 20%通過哥哥；因此哥哥在去程的一小時只看到 12 分鐘的慢動作。回程的一小時，通過哥哥的電磁波則包含上半場的後段 48 分鐘和整個下半場的一小時，他看了 1.8 倍快轉的球賽轉播。

然而，回程時間（哥哥觀測的總波數 X 波長/c）和去程時間（哥哥觀測的總波數 X 波長/c）相同，所以，對哥哥來說雖然轉播速度先慢後快，但是按照蔡先生的時間公式，往返所用的時間是相同的。弟弟所用的時間（弟弟觀測的總波數 X 波長/c）則是固定的轉播速度。

更簡單的計算方法是，由轉播站的固定波長去看哥哥的旅行過程。

不論哥哥用等速度還是變速度，我們在開播以後讓哥哥由轉播站出發，接著任意亂走，只要哥哥在轉播結束時回到轉播站，那麼哥哥所接收到的轉播總波數和弟弟所接收到的轉播總波數“必定”相同。

所以兄弟兩人在轉播開始那個時刻的“冰凍宇宙”和結束時刻的“冰凍宇宙”之間，度過相同的時段。

5-2. 愛因斯坦的錯誤

蔡先生提到，愛因斯坦用火車上的觀測員回頭看月台上的時鐘來說明他自己如何發現觀測員的速度讓時間變慢。

蔡先生引述愛因斯坦的話說：

愛因斯坦說“我坐在高速火車，回頭看月台上的時鐘；當火車越來越快時，鐘的速度變得越來越慢了。當火車速度等於光速時，鐘便停止不動了。”

蔡先生說，“其實愛因斯坦只想了一半。如果他轉頭看下一個月台的鐘，會發現效應相反。對於時間理論，愛因斯坦犯的錯誤是：他沒有先去找尋全宇宙共通的時間計算辦法，就由麥克斯威爾的電磁方程組開始思考時間的真理！於是才想出時間隨觀測者的速度改變流速。”

5-3. 光子是什麼？

蔡先生說，“在狹義相對論發表五十周年的紀念酒會上，愛因斯坦致詞時說：‘五十年前我發現光子，然而，直到今天我們還是不真懂得光子到底是什麼。’時間又過了五十多年，情況還是一樣，我們還是不真懂得光子到底是什麼。”

他說，光是宇宙中最普遍的物理現象。宇宙其他不同時空的智能生物科學家們，他們掌握到的“光效應”也將跟我們所看到的相同。

蔡先生認為，光是宇宙間的共同語言，是宇宙的唯一尺度；思想實驗始於觀察而觀察必須透過光波的傳遞。

雖然蔡先生也和我一樣，沒有明確的描述光子，但是，他用光波的波長，總波數和光速寫出他的時間公式。

5-4. 宇宙秒速

蔡先生認為，如果我們要讓光速在宇宙尺度裡頭等於一，那麼，我們就應該趁這個機會把所有的科學度量全部用“時間”與“長度”來表示。

首先，我們就得把質量用時空單位來表示。也就是說，GM=(V^2)R 裡頭的 G 必須被吸收到速度 V 或半徑 R 裡頭。

蔡先生建議用“1 個宇秒=（（1000G）^（1/2））秒“把“秒速”換算成“宇宙秒速”。

然後，因為光速將由“每秒 299792458 公尺”換算成“每宇秒 299792458x3853.96278 公尺”，大約是“每宇秒移動 1156188834 公里”，所以，必須規定“1 個宇里大約等於 1156188834 公里”。

這樣，我們就有等於一的光速，也就是，“光在 1 宇秒的時間走了 1 宇里的長度”。

既然透過宇秒的安排，質量可以用時空數值來表示，那麼，力和能也就可以全部用時空數值來表示。

於是，我們就可以用時空數值來表示所有的物理度量值。

蔡先生認為，一旦所有物理量都用時空數值去代表，再加上水密度為 1 和第一空間的觀念，那麼，所有物理公式就全部簡化成“速度與光速比”的應用。

這一點和兩個“冰凍宇宙時刻”之間為時間，那個概念，有些類似。

5-5. 蔡先生加油

但是，蔡先生並沒有交代“電荷”如何出現在他的物理公式裡頭，當然，在蔡先生的公式裡頭，也沒有反粒子。

蔡先生的公式也和愛因斯坦的質能互換公式具有相同的缺陷，他們的公式都沒有包括溫度差異。

除了上列的不足，蔡先生硬性寫下了“星體表面溫度”也可以用長度和速度來表現的簡單代換；可是他卻沒有進一步說明。

另外，他說的“重力可以改由盤面公轉速度與光速之比（e）來描述；量子力學裡的電磁力，強核力，弱核力，同樣地也可以用 e 來描述。”其實都只是僵硬的假設。

所以，蔡先生還得加油，把自己的理論解釋清楚。

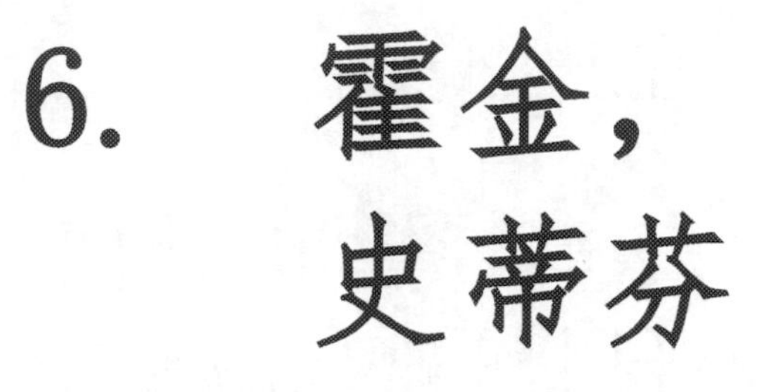

霍金先生名叫史蒂芬，
Stephen Hawking。

在科學界，他的“時間簡史”，A Brief History of Time 是今日世界，物理學家所拿得出來的最後一個里程碑。

那本在 1988 年出版的書，詳細說明自亞里斯多德，伽利略，牛頓，和愛因斯坦以來，人類在物理學上的發展。

那是一本非常完整的物理歷史，因為，該書出版後到 2015 年年初，再也沒有重要而被廣泛討論的物理新知。蔡志忠的反狹相不曾引起共鳴，連湯克雲的引力速度實驗都簡直乏人問津。

6-1. 絕對時空的消逝

在時間簡史第 2 章，空間與時間，他提到在伽利略和牛頓時代的絕對靜止空間，自從愛因斯坦證明了洛侖茲轉換（洛轉）以後，就被否定掉了。

接著他說明絕對時間被否定的關鍵點。

在伽利略和牛頓的時代，對所有慣性移動的觀測員來說，他們所觀測到的物理定律應該相同。然而，當馬克士威的電磁方程組告訴人們“不論光源速度如何改變，電磁波的速率不變”的時候；愛因斯坦卻獨立的大膽假設“對所有慣性移動的觀測員來說，他們所觀測到的光速應該相同。”

霍金先生說，愛因斯坦接著發明了否定絕對時間的狹義相對論（狹相）。因為狹相和洛轉的合作，成功贏得多數物理學家的寵愛，牛頓的絕對時間就消失了。

他說，從此，觀測員的時間計算必須隨著觀測員的慣性速度，依照狹相公式去調整。

依照狹相公式，時間速度因為觀測員本身的速度而異。狹相在 20 世紀征服了大多數物理學家，所以，到了 21 世紀，人類也就正式進入了四維時空的愛因斯坦時代。

6-2. 測不準原理

該書最精彩的是對各種物理發現的簡潔說明。尤其是在第 4 章對測不準原理的解釋。

霍金先生說，如果要預測一個微粒子未來的位置和速度，那麼，人們必須先精確的測量那個微粒子現在的位置和速度。

問題是，測量粒子的位置和速度都靠光子；因此，距離的精密單位長度無法小於所用光子的波長。所以，為了提高對位置觀測的精密度人們需要用高頻率的電磁波；但是，光子的能量越高，對該微粒子速度的影響越大，在實驗室觀測到的微粒子的移動速度也就越不準確。

於是，利用光子來測量粒子的位置和速度，必定無法同時精準。位置越準確，速度就越不準確；反之亦然。

然而，如果您要測量的只是事件的位置和時刻，就沒有問題。

6-3. 無邊界假說

霍金先生在 1982 年以廣相的四唯時空為基礎，推論出宇宙的質能密度有不規則變動的現象；也就是說，這樣的宇宙會變得有些不均勻，逐漸發展成星系。

在廣相的時空裡頭，時間對應一個“類似空間變數”的虛數變數，叫做“虛幻時間”；霍金先生把這個虛幻時間當作歐氏幾何的第四維空間，利用費曼，理察（Richard Feynman）的“路徑積分公式”（或者叫做“總和歷史方法”）對各類的宇宙歷史事件去分析宇宙的量子行為。

他認為其中“時空封閉”的那一類宇宙模型，好像地球表面，那種沒有起點也沒有終點的宇宙是最自然的宇宙模型。那就是他的“無邊界假說”。

後來他在 1985 年認為當宇宙膨脹到最大點以後，時間會開始向過去移動，走回歷史。可是他很快就被他的兩個學生說服，認錯。

也就是說，“無邊界假說”主張，即使宇宙縮收，人們仍然只記得過去，而沒有任何未來的印象。

關於“無邊界假說”的詳細說明，您可以參考在 1995 年出版的奧瑟曼先生（Robert Osserman）的書“宇宙的詩篇”， Poetry of the Universe。

6-4. 霍金輻射

在他 2013 年的自傳第 13 章，霍金認為他在 1974 年提出的霍金輻射理論應當獲得諾貝爾物理獎。

由於那個立足於“廣相理論”上頭的霍金輻射理論，從 1991 年到 1997 年，霍金先生與其他科學家之間引發了多次的“黑洞打賭事件”。

現在，人們不知道究竟廣相會不會因為“狹相突然失去洛轉的支持”而被改寫成“沒有洛轉的廣相”。

如果廣相改寫了，霍金輻射也只好跟著廣相而改寫。

卻不知，誰來改寫廣相。

6-5. 兩次可惜的機會

“時間簡史”把霍金先生“黑洞並不很黑”的理論說明得很清楚，它也介紹了弦理論。那是一本非常難得的物理近代史。

但是，很可惜，他對於圖 2.2 到圖 2.3 的說明裡頭所提到的 300 公尺和 600 公尺光殼沒有繼續想像下去；浪費了一個機會。

在 4-8 那一節，我提到，那個一直擴大的光皮的球心正是一個絕對靜止空間的靜止點。因為，在指定時刻只發光一次以後，燈泡可能會“離開”發光時刻的那一個宇宙中的指定點，然而，不論光殼變得多大，那一組光殼的球心，永遠是宇宙空間裡頭那一個原來的指定點。那是一個宇宙的絕對靜止點。

接著，在圖 2.7 到圖 2.8 的說明裡頭，霍金先生說，按照牛頓的萬有引力公式，可以推論出引力的速度必須是“無限快”。

我認為，雖然牛頓的公式沒有交代動態的情況，但是，那個靜態引力公式也沒有主張引力的速度是“無限快”，牛頓只是對引力的速度不做猜測而已；所以，霍金先生這個認定也算是該書比較可惜的一個，人云亦云的推論。

如果在寫書的時候，他用“重力的速度等於光速”去改良牛頓的引力公式，那麼，霍金先生就比湯克雲更早使用同一種方法去說明水星近日點的移動問題。霍金又浪費了一個好機會。

霍金先生對一個公式做出主觀推論，為什麼不好呢？

我再舉一個例子來說明。好比從“都卜勒效應”的公式可以推論出以下“頻率不變”的結果：“只要光源和觀測員之間的距離保持固定，不論它們如何移動，觀測員所觀測到的頻率不變”。

如果光源和觀測員它們只作等速度移動，這是對的；然而，在變速的時段，觀測員必定可以測量到頻率的變異。我們卻不能夠硬說都卜勒先生的公式“主張”即使在加速的時候，觀測員所觀測到的頻率仍然不變，對不對？

都卜勒先生只是沒有進一步說明，在加速的情況會有哪些相關的變動細節而已。如果人們對都卜勒效應做加速度分析：當它們朝光源方向做等速度移動時，觀測員會比靜止時早一些錄到波峰；而朝反方向移動，會晚一些錄到波峰；所以在加速的時段，觀測員會記錄到些微的頻率變化。

但是，都卜勒效應公式主要是用在等速度的情況，所以，加速時的變化只在精密實驗時必須注意。都卜勒先生沒有特別提起加速度的情況。就好像牛頓引力公式主要是用在星球運轉，所以，只有在需要精密計算的水星軌道才必須注意引力的速度問題。

牛頓先生並沒有特別提到引力的速度。

7. 湯克雲

在 2012 年 12 月 1 日正式發表的湯克雲“引力速度實驗”就漂亮的完善了牛頓的“萬有引力定律”。

湯克雲的引力速度實驗終於在 2009 年 7 月和 8 月中進行的多地點多次數的現場觀測取得可靠數據，而在 2011 年 8 月 15 日首次發表觀測的實驗結果。那個結果就是“引力的速度等於光速”。

請參考以下報導：
http://blog.sciencenet.cn/blog-51667-646834.html 和 http://link.springer.com/article/10.1007%2Fs11434-012-5603-3。

牛頓引力定律只適用於不動的兩個物體，而湯克雲把它擴充到移動的兩個物體上，從而讓“動態引力公式”取代了“廣相公式”的主要功能。

湯克雲用他的“動態引力公式”一個一個計算水星近日點運動、光頻引力紅移、光線引力偏折以及雷達回波延遲的數值。他的計算結果與觀測結果非常符合，也和愛因斯坦的廣相所宣稱的結果相同。

所以我說，“廣相公式”的主要功能被湯克雲的“動態引力公式”給取代了。

人類還有許多無法解釋的科學謎題。以下是我所看過的一些大謎題。我相信，總有一天，人們會把它們搞定。

7-1. 哈伯定律

哈伯先生名叫愛德溫，Edwin Hubble，(1989-11-20 到 1953-9-28)。他的“哈伯定律”，Hubble’s Law，是一個天文學的大謎題。

哈伯定律說，離我們越遠的星系，遠離我們的速度越快。

到目前為止，我們不知道為什麼現在的宇宙會這樣擴張，我們也不知道很久以後，宇宙會不會縮收。我們不知道，宇宙如何開始， 如何結束；我們也不知道人類如何開始， 如何結束。

我們知道，太陽會逐漸冷卻而且，地球好像就要面臨一次冰河期。也許，還有可能地磁翻轉，乃至於慧星或超大隕石撞地球。

第四個問題，是人類對空氣，水和土壤的污染。

總之，地球不是一個永恆的住所。

如果人類想要延續億萬年，那麼，以上目前所知道的四個問題都必須解決。

研究以下四個學問也許可以幫助人類解決以上四個問題。

7-2. 反物質

1927 年 12 月，英國物理學家狄拉克先生，Paul Dirac，提出了電子的相對論方程式。

他在等式中發現除了一般正能量之外的負能量。狄拉克認為真空狀態中充滿了負能量電子的「海」，稱作狄拉克之海。真實的電子會填補這些海中具有正能量的部分，就像一個個的島。

衍伸這個想法，狄拉克發現海中的這些「島」應該具有正電荷。起初他認為這是質子，但是有人指出這些島應該具有和電子相同的質量。在 1931 年狄拉克先生接受建議，並且正式給這些島命名為“反電子”。

後來在 1932 年 8 月 2 日，由美國物理學家安德森先生，Carl Anderson，在實驗中證實了反電子的存在，並且把它叫做正電子。

1933 年狄拉克先生預測反質子的存在，1955 年就被證實。

接著是各種反物質的合成和正電子的量產，但是，科學家們還沒有在大自然中發現天生的反粒子。

為什麼沒有天生的反粒子或反物質？到目前為止，我們還不知道答案。

7-3. 光子

為什麼每一個光子的速度都一樣？當光子改變頻率的時候，它如何調整波長？它如何在能量被轉走的那一剎那突然的改變波長？它需要一段時間去反應嗎？如果需要一段時間，那麼，在那一段時間裡頭，光子變換波長的詳細過程是哪幾個？光子有沒有帶著中和（等量）的微電荷？光子是不是無所不在？

到目前為止，關於光子的這些問題，我們都還不知道答案。

如果不論多遠的地方都有光子，那麼，我們的宇宙就無限大而“大爆炸的宇宙開端假說”就不能夠成立。

而且，如果不論多遠的地方都有光子，那麼，質能就因為無遠弗屆的光子而占據無限遠的空間。在那種情況下，物理也就和數學在“無限大”的地方會合了。

7-4. Muon 介子的衰變

為什麼快速移動的介子，像是 muon 介子，會有較長的半衰期？到目前為止，我們還不知道答案。

7-5. 飛碟 （UFO）

人類從麥田圈，Crop Circles ，可以明白外星人，Saucerman ，的存在。可是，到目前為止我們還不知道，為什麼飛碟能夠移動自如？

我們也不知道，究竟外星人住在哪裡？

根據天文觀測結果，我們知道，宇宙裡頭的東西大約有百分之一是我們能夠偵測的質能，百分之九是我們無法偵測的暗質能（黑洞那一類的東西），而其他百分之九十則是我們根本無法想像的東西。

也許，外星人在那百分之九十的東西裡頭，可以把飛碟操縱得比較自由些。也許可以相當接近光速？

到目前為止，我們還不知道答案。

8. 距離相對論

在“玫瑰與幸福的狹義相對論”那本書裡頭，作者介紹了“距離轉換”（距轉）和“距離相對論”（距相），並且希望它們在經過改善以後可以取代洛轉和狹相。

在距轉和距相裡頭，時空是絕對的。

雖然距轉公式非常複雜，但是，距轉的概念卻十分簡單：

觀測到的事件時刻一定不會比真實的事件時刻更早，而且，越遠的觀測員所記錄的事件時刻越晚。

距轉只是把這樣一個簡單，卻非常實際，的概念加入“伽利略轉換”（伽轉）裡頭，讓理論上無限多觀測員的伽轉，改善為實際上只有兩個觀測員的距轉。

在電腦發達的 21 世紀，天文學家們還是很有機會從距轉裡頭挖出金礦。如果科技能夠奈米化，那麼，距轉還可能加惠人們的日常生活。

8-1. 軟件和事實

電腦科技本來包括軟件和硬件，但是，由於銜接事實的軟件永遠跟不上事實的變化和需求，所以軟件的發展就遠遠落後事實的變化。

在周邊配件和電腦主機之間的界面很簡單，把輸出和輸入的雙向代碼牽好就解決了。可是軟件和事實的配合可複雜多了。

最麻煩的事實變化是“法律”。一旦法律變動，政府和相關公司的作業軟體往往無法及時跟上。第二麻煩的事實變化是“組織結構”。一旦組織改組或合併，機構的軟體也必定要做或多或少的更新。第三麻煩的事實變化是“商品絕種”。從二十世紀中期開始，商品變動漸漸加快；如果有某一種類的商品完全退出市場，軟件就不得不做局部更新。

資訊的儲存和讀寫媒介，由甲骨，竹簡，絹帛，圖書，經過電腦儲存的硬碟，軟碟，拷貝帶，光碟，進展到現在的快閃記憶體。

資訊的儲存和讀寫方式也由口述，圖示，文字，錄像，錄音，動畫，錄影，而發展到電腦特效和立體電影。

有許多電腦相關的媒介都只在歷史中存活很短的歲月。

第四麻煩的事實變化是“既無固定時刻也無發展方向的偶發安全事件”像是病毒，停電，主機當機和駭客入侵等等安全問題。

然而，一個加入越多保全功能的硬件或軟件，它那主要作業的工作效率就越差。因為硬件要花時間做備用儲存而防毒軟件要花時間檢查準備進入和已經儲存的資料和程式。

最隱密的麻煩是，事實上，在 21 世紀，電腦已經成為人類的命脈。幾乎人類所有的買賣都依賴電腦。

尤其在大都會，沒有買賣，就沒有三餐；所以電腦已經是城市居民賴以維生的必要工具。

就算領退休金住在鄉下，退休金也依靠電腦發放給銀行；就算退休金是用支票發放，銀行沒有電腦也無法接收支票。對不對?

這個幾乎是隱身的麻煩，已經因為手機的普及與深入而融合到人們的生活裡頭。

在 2015 年人們對於電腦的依賴已經無法回頭。

8-2. 臨時流程

由於事實的變動完全沒有規則可循，所以軟件既有的程式往往不再適用。

如果稍微修改軟件就能夠應變，那麼，人們可以製定一些“臨時流程”，去牽就過時的軟件，去符合新的事實要求；然後慢慢等待軟件的更新。

如果軟件需要重新寫過，那麼，還得看公司有沒有經費去鹹魚翻身，東山再起。

一個軟件的使用者越多，訓練和使用“臨時流程”或“新軟體”所花費的人工就越多，出錯的機會也跟著越大。所以，聯邦政府的臨時作業流程是成本最高的“臨時流程”，因為，她顧用的員工最多。

8-3. 和諧物理世界

洛轉，狹相和廣相組成了一個物理科學的"臨時流程"。然而，因為認真使用這個"臨時流程"的人數（最多只是所有的物理學者）只占人類一個很小很小的比例所以這個"臨時流程"的問題並不嚴重，甚至可以不管它。

然而，這個一百多年的"臨時"實在也是夠長的了。

希望科學家們能夠早日明白原子鐘在不同環境會改變速度的"真正原因"，那麼，物理學者就可以停止那個廣相的"臨時流程"，而重返那個只有動態"牛頓物理"和新興"量子理論"的和諧物理世界。

9. 兩個必須解開的矛盾

1760 年工業革命以後，科學知識迅速成長，先後造就了強盛一時的英國，德國，日本和美國。

此外，科學還在 1912 年摧毀了中國的最後一個皇朝。所以在 20 世紀，科學是人類最熱衷的學問。進入 21 世紀，科技雖然控制了人類的生計，教育和娛樂；但是，科學卻已經被民主給綁架了。

1776 年民主政治在美國誕生，卻在第二次世界大戰以後才傳遍全球。

進入 21 世紀，全人類都知道美國這個民主政治政府，而且，目前絕大多數的政府已經建立或多或少的民主管道。在人類歷史中，專制政府往往無法持久；但是，民主政府不但沒有工作效率而且後知後覺，甚至於，不知不覺。

9-1. 凡者隨機而行

中國有一句話說，聖者先機而動，賢者見機而變，凡者隨機而行，愚者失機而悔。

所謂民主政治就是投票表決，也就是占多數的凡者當家做主。在一個民主政府結構中，人民票選各級首長；而遇到有爭議的法律條款，就公投決定。

凡人的特點是看不到機會，無法見機而變；當然就更加無法先機而動。

凡人是跟在機會後面走的，隨波逐流的人群。

凡人是比那些跟不上潮流的愚人更容易生存，但是，凡人當家做主一定不如聖賢當家做主。因為，解決一個問題，不論問題大小繁簡，最好是先機而動，其次是見機而變。當人們隨機而行的時候，問題已經惡化。

凡人，不可能又要做主，又不解決問題，對不對？

這是一個人們必須解開的矛盾。

雖然不容易，人們卻必須找到比民主政府更理想的政府結構，讓聖賢有更好的機會掌政。

9-2. 統計學

科學知識是包含公式的知識；既然全球瘋迷科學，教師們就用統計學把有可能被統計加工的知識都被統計學給勉強的科學化了。

當然，還是有許多好學問沒有辦法被統計學加工。然而，自從個人電腦進入市場以後，幾乎所有學問或多或少，都被電腦化了。於是，經過一百年的科學洗禮，和六十多年的電腦處理，科學知識就在人們不知不覺間取代了知識。

那些無法統計處理的知識，好比哲學，棋藝，歌曲，樂器，舞蹈，書法，繪畫，雕刻，中醫，武術，騎射，等等；雖然也能夠透過電腦網路交流傳播，但是它們實在和賺錢的距離相去太遠，所以，很少人參與活動，很難逐代傳遞下去。

那些知識，包括哲學，也就逐漸淪為娛樂技藝。

9-3. 所謂知識

知識是此時此地，你所用得上的歷史資訊加上你現在的邏輯能力。邏輯能力包括基本的推理能力和進階的想像能力。

所以，知識的內容，由個人的資質與努力決定。

知識是累積的。

一個人，依靠邏輯把事件給記錄在腦海裡。事件記錄得越多或者越合理，在面對抉擇的時刻，往往越容易“及時”做出“好”的決定。

進入 21 世紀，越來越多的人利用電腦來協助他們抉擇；因為，快速利潤已經分秒必爭。

9-4. 好的抉擇

人生，其實就是一個接一個的抉擇而已。

那麼，什麼樣的抉擇算是一個好的抉擇呢？

依賴電腦化的統計資訊所做成的抉擇是比較科學化的抉擇。然而，能夠統計的資訊，必須是有數量的或者是有價錢的；因此，電腦化的好抉擇應該只適用於商業（有價）和科學（有量）這兩個範圍。

雖然如此，由於在 20 世紀的一百年間，商人已經從第四等人晉升為第一等人，所以，只要電統計資訊足夠客觀，在 21 世紀，電腦化的好抉擇卻已經被用來代表所有的好抉擇。

如今，幾乎人人都想做個成功的商人。

9-5. 利潤

商人，就是追求利潤的人。

在士農工商的時代，農人提供食物，工人提供工具而文人傳承知識；唯獨商人，在大都市裡頭經手買賣，唯利是圖，才被人們看輕身分。

所謂無巧不成商，無爭不成王；雖然言過其實，但是，在都市已經形成又不需要全民教育的時代，識字還是奢侈的學問。在那個時期，人民大多以務農為生，自食其力；所以，沒有巧變不成大利，沒有爭戰不得天下；卻也是當時的實情。

中國人罵奸商，罵庸君，一直罵到清朝。然後，西方文化進入中國，商人的地位才一路爬升，終於升上第一等人的位置。

在 1776 年 7 月 4 日美國發表獨立宣言以後，美國總統的誕生，既不是家傳也不需要戰爭。進入 21 世紀，全世界只有少數地方，以戰爭決定國王。商人，逐漸掌控了法律，決定了道德的底線；而政府，既必須配合商人的需求，官員也多與商人共同謀利。簡單的說，21 世紀已經是金錢掛帥的世紀。

除了以戰爭決定國王的地方，人們大多以營利為努力的目標。

然而，在“士農工商”轉變為“商工農士”的一百年裡頭，不但人類的人生目標從“立功，立德，立言”轉變為“立業”；人類的人生目的也從“情義傳家”轉變為“舒適生活”。

在民主地區，人們的共識就是營利。

9-6. 情義傳家

在短短的一百年裡頭，人類的人生目標由 19 世紀的“三立”集中為“一立”，而人類的人生目的也從“情義傳家”轉變為簡單的“舒適生活”。

在 19 世紀，人生在世只有兩個字，就是情與義。在私有情；在公重義。如今情義二字的字義並沒有改變，只是，成全情義的勇氣不見了。

在 19 世紀，凡人的人生目標是成家立業。如今，因為“傳家”的人生目的不見了，所以，“成家”的人生目標也就跟著消失了。

進入 21 世紀，科學是人們的主要學問。立業需要科學，舒適生活更需要科學。科學讓人們的價值觀改變了。

9-7. 舒適生活

簡單的人生目的和目標讓人平靜。立業和舒適生活看起來既實際又簡單。然而，在營利的商業社會，這個看似簡單的立業和舒適生活並不容易做到，而且有個必須解開的矛盾藏在裡頭。

首先，立業有兩個方向。一個是，有個自己的事業，當老闆；另一個是，有個謀生的能力，有飯碗。

在 21 世紀，電腦控制多數的生產，運輸和經銷作業，為了應付市場變動，裁員成為大公司的經營常態；於是有了急需員工的時刻，臨時工行業也就應勢而起。

朝不保夕的臨時工實在不像一個飯碗。然而，多數公司以電腦為暗箱，員工只負責按鈕；所以越來越多的工作，根本就是三兩下就可以完訓上陣。也所以，找個非臨時工的飯碗，難。

自己當老闆呢？

市場因為運輸方便，已經失去邊界。商品因為科技更新，已經無法持久。在這個多變的環境，自己當老闆，需要在變化中看出商機。所以，難。

立業難，舒適生活也就不容易。

這個看似簡單的"立業目標"和"舒適目的"如果達到了，卻還有一個必須解開的矛盾藏在每一個人的人生目標和人生目的裡頭。

9-8. 智仁勇

除了看看電視新聞和娛樂節目以外，人們大都愛看好的故事。不論是書，漫畫，電影還是連續劇，那些智仁勇的故事，只要表達生動，必定大受歡迎。

在網路上的電玩虛擬世界，人們還可以變身主角，幹下感天動地的大事。

就像白日夢，只是，現代的白日夢可以在“電腦虛擬的世界”顯現出來，更加令人愛不釋手。

是的，商人也是人；所以，也有智仁勇的表現。然而，人不是商人；爭取一時的利潤只需要一小部分的智，所以，“成功的商人”這個成功的目標偏離了“智仁勇”這個成功的中心點。

智仁勇表現了真善美，有價值的事物卻只占一小部分真。商人這個身分，失掉許多真，不考慮善而害怕勇。

9-9. 實用事件

在白日夢裡頭，人們幻想自己是一個勇於承擔私情或公義的“好人”。但是，在真實世界裡頭，商人最不勇敢。商人總認為金錢萬能所以不必勇敢。偶而做個不敢承擔私情或公義的“壞人”，在商人眼中，是為了謀利所“必須”採取的權宜之計。商人既然是追求利潤的人，為了利潤，親友是受保人的實驗首選，也是老鼠會會友的必然對象；損害私情在所難免。然而，更嚴重的問題是破壞公義；因為商業做大以後，官商勾結勢在必行。

利潤這兩個字，基本上讓同類產品無法“雙贏”，讓同行之間很難長久共存；只因為利潤是越多越好，沒有上限。

人們既然已經把“成功的商人”當作 21 世紀的模範，以上好人和壞人（夢想和事實）的矛盾也就成為“一個現代人必須解開的矛盾”。

身處事件氾濫的 21 世紀，選讀資訊已經變成一個人人需要面對的問題。沒有時間吸收蜂擁而至的超量資訊，怎麼辦？成人有這個問題，教育當然無法避開同樣的問題。

我認為

人類應當傳遞的資訊至少有兩類，一類是，美妙藝術作品的詳細相關資訊；另一類是，偉大事件的詳細歷史。

這兩類資訊，尤其是偉大事件的詳情，不一定和科學知識相關，但是，它們和人生目的息息相關。我們需要常常研讀偉人所完成的大小事件的詳細過程。

我把這兩類資訊叫做實用事件。

傳播實用事件的作用也許十分緩慢，但是，我相信，這個動作有希望逐步化解現代人的矛盾。

20 世紀最大的矛盾莫過於被神化的 E=mc^2。愛因斯坦沒說“在什麼溫度下”可以使用該公式，也沒說該公式不含熱能。即使考慮了溫度，科學還是無法說明所有的“動”。由動體的大小，我們可以把動分為 4 級。星行和行星級， 地球附近質量級，地球附近能量級和意念級。在意念級，意念之動，如天馬行空，科學望塵莫及。

10. 西台已立社

西台助立社（STEPA）計劃書

西台助立社是一個即將成立的社團。英文名稱叫做 Seattle-Taiwanese Entrepreneurs-Promoting Association(STEPA)。

在我的構想中，社員由西雅圖地區已經站穩腳步的台灣人組成。沒有辦公室，不必交會費，會長任期由會長自己決定，會員名單在網路上。

STEPA 的目的是集思廣益，增加工作機會。

那是己立立人的意思；既然已立，就開始立人吧。

STEPA 的做法是，成立各種子社團，分別尋找既有的公司為主要投資人，成立各種特定的營利公司。所謂特定，指的是，薪資制度和利潤分配。子社團，如下頁例。

薪資制度：廉能管理制

基層工作人員的時薪和福利比照該地區類似工作的平均待遇。如果有領班，因為領班除了基層工作，還得訓練新手，推動變更的流程，處理緊急狀況；所以，其待遇為所屬員工最高待遇的 105%。領班以上所有經理人員的待遇一律為所有“直接”管轄的人員的平均待遇；一律為時薪制。

利潤分配：分紅不超過 15%

最先 5 年，股東分紅不超過利潤的 5%；其次 5 年，不超過 10%；然後，不超過 15%。

10-1. 西雅圖好妙社（SEAA）

選一個西雅圖，台人或華人，報紙負責人或有擔當社長經驗的人擔任社長；其他社員為輔，我為連絡人成立“西雅圖好妙社”Seattle virtuous-Events and wonderful-Arts Association（SEAA）。

社團目標是利用只報導“好妙事件”的營利周刊，給更多“編輯人”和“翻譯人”帶來溫飽的工作機會；這個目標包括三個階段：

第一階段，由我尋找創社社員，然後由社長申報財團法人。社長出資 52%（約$5200.00），其他創社社員均攤 48%（約 $480.00 x 10)。

第二階段，找一家大規模的華人出版公司在西雅圖或台灣，成立好妙周刊社，出版好妙周刊。目前可能的選項為“Taiwan News”，大紀元時報和天下雜誌等等。實行辦法和步驟如下頁開始的附件，暫且以天下雜誌為例子。

出版 GeGa Weekly ，報導好妙事件。

Great virtuous-Events and Grate wonderful-Arts Weekly Inc.
大美好事件以及大奇妙藝術周刊社，

(GeGaWI) 好妙周刊社

專門報導美妙藝術品的相關內容和偉大事件的詳細歷史。
包括和事件有關的時間，地點，人物，器材，以及事件的詳細經過。有好事件的好東西，優先報導。

第三階段，把 GeGaWI 賣給 Google 或其他全球性的大公司，附屬於 GeWeekly 或 XeWeekly, 進行全球化。

10-2. The Proposal of GeGaWI

A proposal of GeGa Weekly

好妙周刊草案

by SEAA（西雅圖好妙社）

Great virtuous-Events and Grate wonderful-Arts Weekly Inc.

GeGaWI, 好妙周刊社

Purpose:

The main purpose of creating GeGaWI and its branch offices is to create decent editor's and translator's jobs for more and more people via publishing GeGa Weekly. 成立 GeGaWI 利用好妙周刊提供溫飽的編輯工作。

What is GeGa Weekly?

GeGa Weekly is a weekly newspaper about PRACTICAL news. All news provided by PeWeekly must be at least 7 days old. The report must be practically useful and must base on fact, promote kindness and justice, 守真，揚善，求義.

How GeGa Weekly work?

The workers at GeGa Weekly believe that they will make mistakes so that when subscribers correct mistakes in reports, those actions will receive some editing reward-points. The report summaries are free to everyone but the details are available for subscribers only.

A common guide line:

Chinese people believe that people should focus on current life and current world only. They try to make the current world an ideal world, named "DaTong-ShiJie", where their offspring may enjoy. They don't know how long can souls (or ghosts) live.

Hindu and Buddhist believe in transmigration of souls and wish their souls could escape from the current troublesome world to a peaceful land. Catholic, Christian and Moslem believe in one God and wish their souls will stay with God in the heaven after they die.

Although people believe in different religious teachings and wish for different future of their souls, they all agree on the common guide line that people should find the truth, do good things and appreciate beauties, especially internal beauties.
人類的共同行為方針：尋真，行善，賞美，尤其是內在美。

Plans:

Plan 1: GeGa Weekly will provide free commercial for one to three selected business partners like IKEA and I-Mei Foods Co., LTD (IMEI) …(to be decided). GeGa Weekly will also provide a small area for paid commercials and GeGa Weekly will verify the commercials before put them on the website. All branch offices of GeGa Weekly will verify all commercials too.

Plan 2: At the first five years, GeGa Weekly and its branch offices will distribute local practical news related to science, politics/laws, and arts, especially NEW events related to HARMONIC HUMAN SOCIETIES, and try to support themselves by all kinds of verified commercials and the membership income from subscribers.

Plan 3: Five years later, they will start to design some local projects to enhance local harmonic environments with other related groups. GeGa Weekly will also try to sell itself to Google or other influential international company with the condition that Epoch Times will be one of the three business partners which will occupy the commercial position of education as shown in the following figure.

Commercial Income:

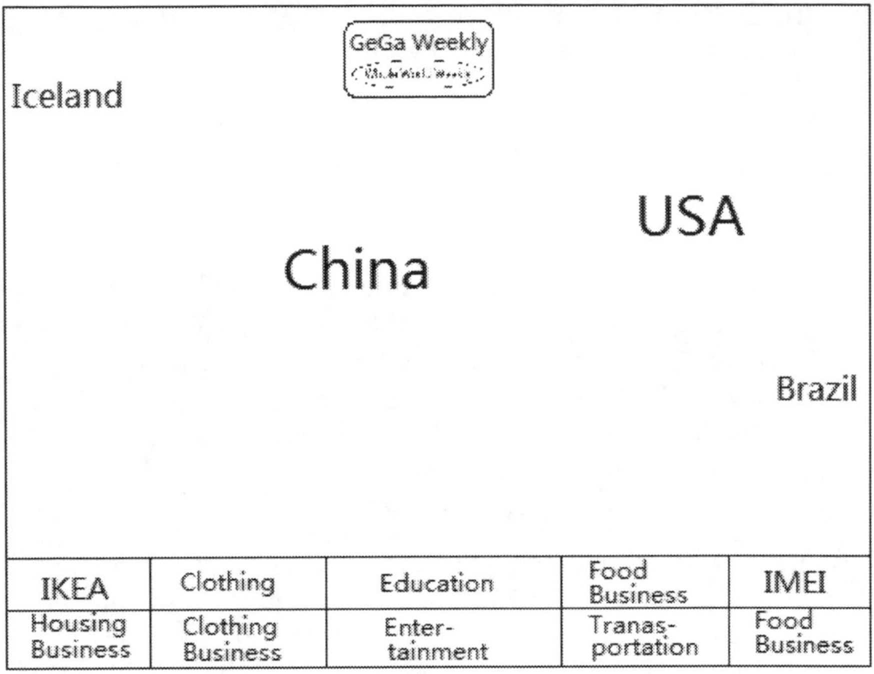

GeGa Weekly

Iceland

USA

China

Brazil

IKEA	Clothing	Education	Food Business	IMEI
Housing Business	Clothing Business	Enter-tainment	Tranas-portation	Food Business

Besides subscribers' payment GeGa Weekly will use the bottom space which is 20% (or 25%, 33% to be enlarged) of the whole screen to sell commercials. At the upper left corner, 1/10 of the bottom space is reserved for IKEA, at the upper right corner, 1/10 of the bottom space is reserved for IMEI. Besides IKEA, two 1/10 of the bottom spaces are open to clothing related businesses. Under IKEA, there is one 1/10 space open to housing related businesses. In the center area, the upper 1/10 space is open to education related business and the 1/10 space under it is open to entertainment related business. Tow 1/10 spaces connected to IMEI are open to food related businesses and the last 1/10 space is open to transportation related business.

However, all the 10 available spaces are all open in the homepages of branch offices in related areas. The reserved areas for IKEA and IMEI will not show up on the local homepages unless they pay for it.

The representatives of IKEA and IMEI may work at GeGa Weekly when the branch offices of GeGa Weekly is more than 50 and at that time, the commercial area will increase to 25% of the total homepage for all offices in GeGa Weekly Inc. The representatives of IKEA and IMEI will update their own homepages. When the number of branch offices is more than 1000, the commercial space will increase to 33% of the total homepage for all offices in GeGa Weekly.

Homepages

Each sub-branch office of GeGa Weekly will show on the map of related branch offices. The map occupies 4/5 (or ¾, 2/3 to be reduced) of homepage. After users selected a branch office, the home page of that branch office will have its sub-branch offices shown on its local map. Branch offices of GeGa Weekly will not display IKEA and IMEI commercials but they may select one to three local businesses or groups as their business partners.

They will verify all commercials before put commercials on their homepages. A sub-branch office may have sub-sub-branch offices if the situation is appropriate.

The upper 4/5 (or ¾, 2/3 to be reduced) of the homepage of GeGa Weekly will be the map of the world so that viewers can select the area or location they like to see practical news. For practical news of the whole world, just select the Whole World Weekly logo at the center top area. Yes, GeGa Weekly will provide ONLY practical (trying to be useful) news of the real world.

The upper 4/5 (or ¾, 2/3 to be reduced) of the homepage of each branch office and sub-branch office will be the map of the related local area so that viewers can select the area or location they like to see practical news, for practical news of the whole related area, just select the logo of Whole Local Weekly at the center top area of related homepages.

After viewers selected a location, the following categories will show up with key words of one to twenty events on the right side. The screen function keys are located at the middle of left column.

Truth Science	Physics	Matter-Energy, Location, Motion	(1 to 3)
	Biopology	Selection , Surviving, Multiplication	(1 to 3)
Kindness Politics	Food / Clothing	Related events (people, time, location, objects, summary & details)	(1 to 10)
Function KEYS	Housing / Trans-portation	Related events (people, time, location, objects, summary & details)	(1 to 20)
(Laws / Time)	Education / Enter-tainment	Related events (people, time, location, objects, summary & details)	(1 to 8)
Justice Art	Painting / Literature	Related history (people, time, location, summary & details)	(1 to 5)
	Broadcast / Video	Related history (people, time, location, summary & details)	(1 to 5)
Commercials			

真 (物理，生理)，善 (食衣，住行，育樂)，義 (圖文，影音)
When viewers select one of the key words, the event summary will display and all key words will move to 1/5 of the left screen. The summary will occupy 4/5 of the upper area starting from the selected one and following by the summaries of next events. In function keys area, there will be up and down arrow to move it.

The viewer can also use the squeezed key words to select different summaries.

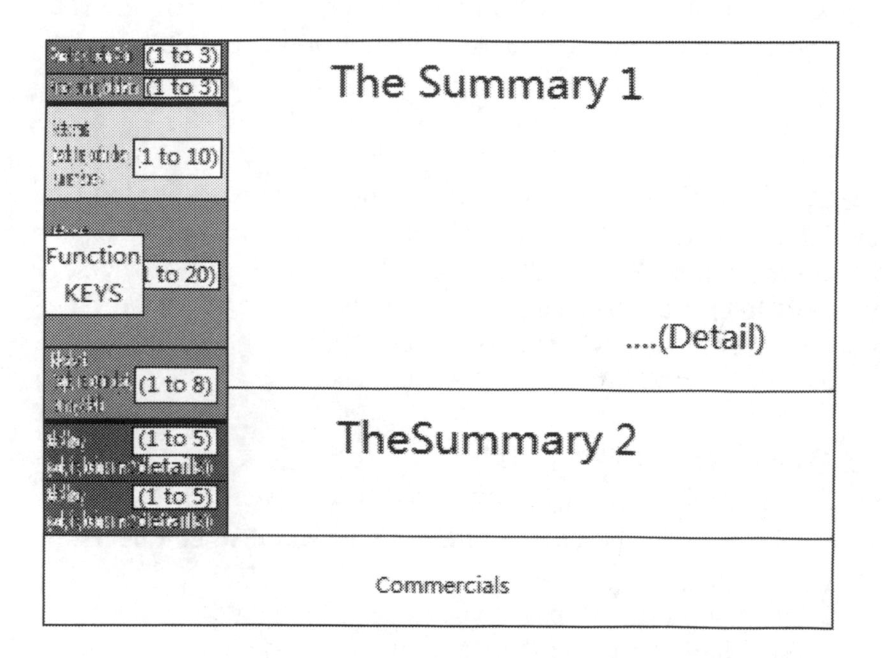

When subscriber click the (details) at the end of each summary, the details of the event will display with source links of related websites. Editors at GeGa Weekly will rewrite all the summary and details of each event. When a non-subscriber click the (details), the subscription information will pop up.

Partners:

The starting partners will be Commonwealth Magazine (CM), IKEA, IMEI and Seattle virtuous-Events and wonderful-Arts Association（SEAA）SEAA will provide 0.1% or 1% of initial fund and each of CM, IKEA and IMEI will provide 33.3% or 33% of the initial fund, the percentage will be decided.

There will be seven workers when GeGa Weekly starts. Four of them will come from retired workers of CM: one CEO, one Logistic Manager, one Chief Editor and one IT Manager. IKEA and IMEI should assign a contact worker from their Public Relation (PR) departments to handle the free 1/10 space at the main homepage of GeGa Weekly.

SEAA will be the coordinator 連絡人 and the worker to establish the Seattle branch in the future. The wage system as well as how to distribute profits are all written in the charter. The stockowners will vote to change the charter based on the percentages of their holding stocks. Here is a draft of the charter.

A draft of the charter:

This draft of the charter for GeGa Weekly will be finalized by the board members and be voted in the meeting of all stockholders.

1. The definition of practical news, will be voted by the ongoing board members and the board members will be elected by the meeting of all stockholders.
2. The wage system is very simple, frontline workers will be paid average wage and benefits of same kind job at related local areas. A lead worker is a frontline worker who also provide on-job training to other frontline workers. If there is a lead worker, the lead worker will receive 110% of the average wage and benefits from all frontline workers under the lead worker. All the managers are paid by wage as well. A manager receives the average wage and benefits of all workers directly report to that manager. Yes, so simple; everyone is paid by wage and overtime is available for everyone to help adopting changes.
3. The distribution of profits is also very simple, most of the profits go to open new branch offices. In the first five years, no more than 5% of profits should go to investors; in the second five years, no more than 10% of profits should go to investors and after that no more than 15% of profits should go to investors.

How to start GeGa Weekly?

Procedure 1: SEAA needs to talk to the Commonwealth Magazine (CM) first. If CM and SEAA can reach some agreement then CM and SEAA will contact IKEA and IMEI for their input regarding the initial investment amount. If CM and SEAA should find another investors to replace IKEA or IMEI, CM may provide a list of potential businesses to invite.

Procedure 2: After investors are ready, GeGa Weekly may rent an office space within CM and CM will assign four retired workers as board members of GeGa Weekly to work with me to draft the charter.

Procedure 3: The next step is the draft of charter should be presented to the stockholders' meeting for approval. After that, the first version of the definition of practical/useful news will be decided by the board members.

After that, the IT Manager will try to design the homepage, the CEO and Chief Editor will try to collect sources of news, the Logistic Manager will prepare the hardware of the rented office and SEAA will coordinate with all of them regarding how to organize the practical news all over the world on the website so that people will like to visit the website continuously. Subscribers can also order paper version of GeGa Weekly.

Procedure 4: The next step is the CEO will call IKEA and IMEI for their input about the homepage. The Chief Editor and SEAA will start to group some news in last year and last month together as samples to attract potential customers of paid commercials.

To report practical/useful good news truly and interestingly is the ongoing key issue to attract subscribers and commercial customers.

If it is possible, CM could open a branch offices in Seattle, USA to start the US branch at the same time.

Procedure 5: Then, CM will create a big icon at the homepage for GeGa Weekly after GeGa Weekly has received deposits for all of the 8/10 available commercial spaces at homepage. After that, GeGa Weekly is officially established.

Procedure 6: The next goal is to create American branch office if not started yet and SEAA will work on it. At that time, or, 2 years later, if the American branch already opened with Taiwan headquarters, the summary will come with pronunciation.

Tiny APA fonts will be put beneath each word of the summaries. This will be a big jump of GeGa Weekly, people can use it as a tool of learning Chinese and English languages. The screen will allow split-windows so that same summary can be displayed by two windows, side by side, of different languages with APA to mark pronunciations of both languages. APA will be extended to cover all main languages. Currently APA can cover English, Chinese, Taiwanese, Hakka, Japanese, Korean and Spanish.

Then, if it is successful, GeGa Weekly will open three more branches, Hong Kong branch, Japan branch and Korea branch.

After the company is established like that, GeGa Weekly can try to sell itself to Google or other big international company and each GeGa Weekly offices will reduce to branch offices of GeWeekly (Google Events Weekly Inc. 谷歌事件周刊) or XeWeekly and CM can be one of three starting partners. ET could occupy the center 1/10 space for educational businesses on the homepage of GeWeekly or XeWeekly if ET wishes to do so.

Three Steps:

The first step is in Traditional Chinese with optional translation to Simplified Chinese and American English only. This is when GeGaWI has offices in Taiwan only.

The second step starts with the American branch office or two years later if American branch already opened, each summary will come with APA to mark each word of the summaries. GeGaWI will change logo to include its Chinese name.

The third step will start after APA is accepted and the APA for Hong Kong, Japan and Korea is ready to go. GeGaWI will open three more branches. Then, try to sell itself to Google or some international company.

Why CM will start it?

There are several reasons for 天下雜誌(CM) to start this business, GeGa Weekly, for practical news.

First of all, GeGa Weekly is a good chance for 天下雜誌(CM) to show up on Google's homepage or be promoted by some international company.

Secondly. 天下雜誌(CM) will write PRACTICAL/USEFUL history. GeGa Weekly will focus on the ecology of human societies and extend it to all living creatures.

GeGa Weekly will report an event after one week later so that the report will cover the key point of an event in detail.

For all reported events, if there is a follow up story, it will be reported later on with a link refer to the last related report. GeGa Weekly will try to make all events interesting so that it will be popular and 天下雜誌(CM) will earn money while writing the worldwide practical/useful history.

The third reason is that GeGa Weekly will create more and more decent editing jobs for people in the whole world based on the charter. If CM can help then CM will like to help, I think.
The fourth reason is that GeGa Weekly will provide PRACTICAL news only and CM is the main party which defines PRACTICAL news at the beginning. CM will have a good control on what should be reported.

CM can have 51% of the total investment to control it if it is a better choice for 天下雜誌(CM). In that case, IKEA and IMEI could invest 24% or 24.4% each so that SEAA will invest 1% or 0.2%.

A good timing

Right now, it is a good timing to support I-Mei.

On 2/8/2015, there was an open letter from Luis Ko, the general manager of I-Mei Foods Company, to urge the government to think very carefully about the consequences of giving green lights to the marketing, sale, and planting of genetically modified foods (or GM foods).
http://www.etaiwannews.com/etn/news_content.php?id=2685677
http://www.bbc.co.uk/zhongwen/trad/china/2015/02/150212_twletter_ny_foodsafty

Why SEAA is a right group to start it?

Most members of SEAA are retired so that they have plenty of time to read, discuss and write. Some workers of SEAA are familiar with APA.

Hope CM would work with SEAA after I find a leader for SEAA.

Name phone # email

What I say & do today,
decide my future & define me.

今日的言行，造就明日的我。

讀者不妨另組社團，想辦法儘早解開矛盾。

Phonetic Table

B (Bopomofo), P (Pinyin), 白（白話字） A (APA)

B	ㄅ	ㄆ	ㄇ	ㄈ	ㄉ	ㄊ	ㄋ	ㄌ	ㄍ	ㄎ	ㄏ	(ㄐ	ㄑ	ㄒ)
P	b	p	m	f	d	t	n	l	g	k	h	(j	q	x)
A	b	p	m	f	d	t	n	l	g	k	h	(ds	ts	s)
白	p	ph	m		t	th	n	l	k	kh	h	(chi	chhi	si)

B	ㄓ	ㄔ	ㄕ	ㄖ	ㄗ	ㄘ	ㄙ				ㄚ	ㄛ	ㄜ	ㄝ
P	zh	ch	sh	r	z	c	s				a	o	e	e
A	dR	tR	sR	R	ds	ts	s	B	G	N	a	o	E	e
白					ch	chh	s	b	g	n	a	o	o	e

B	ㄞ	ㄟ	ㄠ	ㄡ	(ㄢ)	ㄣ	(ㄤ)	ㄥ	ㄦ	ㄧ	ㄨ	ㄩ
P	ai	ei	ao	ou	(an)	n	(ang)	ng	er	y i	w u	ü
A	ai	ei	au	ou	(an)	n	(ang)	ng	ER	y i	w u	yu
白	ai		au		(an)	n	(ang)	ng		i	o u	oa oe ui

English word:	cup	hit	book	cat	very	red	zoo	you
Key letter	u	i	oo	a	v	r	z	you
APA letter	A	I	U	ae	v	r	z	iu
白 letter							z	iu

English word:	judge	church	ship	vision	this	thin
Key letter	j	ch	sh	s	th	th
APA letter	dZ	tZ	sZ	Z	D	T

* Tone marks

	1	2	3	4	5	6	7
Bopomofo		/	v	\			
Pinyin	-	/	v	\			
APA	^	/	v	\	-	v-	>
pitch level	Mi	ReMi	Do	MiDo	Do#	DoDo#	Re
active mood	So	MiSo	Do	SoDo	Re	DoRe	Mi

What I say and do today
wat ai sei aend du tU-dei\
decide my future
dI-sai^d mai fyu^tZEr
and define me.
aend dI-fain^ mi

今日的言行
dsin^ R\ dE- yen/ sing/
造就明日的我。
dsau\ dsyou\ ming/ R\ dE- wov

我今仔日所講所做的嘢若
Gwa- gin- a^ zi- so^ gong\ so^ dsEv ev mv nav
決定我的將來也同時
gwad^dingvGwa- e- dsyong-lai/ yav dong- si/
記錄我的靈魂。
gi\ lov Gwa- e- ling- hwn/

A Draft of English Translation
for "The Definition of Spacetime"

I had two purposes in writing this book. The main one was to define the absolute space and the absolute time while the minor one was to point out three conflicts that people must solve.

The first conflict was provided in the chapter 1 and two conflicts were provided in the chapter 9, then I tried to provide a possible solution in the last chapter, chapter 10.

It take long time to translate this book into English, since the materials is quite the same as my earlier books, I will just provide a draft of the translation. There will be some grammar errors and some wrong wordings in this draft; I will try to correct them if this book will print its second edition.

Here is the draft of English translation for this book.

Subtitle:
A Summary of Physics in 2015 for Publics from a Taiwanese.

Preface: Two children argued about the sun
There was a pretty good physical question in a Chinese book published over 2300 years ago. It was a conflict provided by the author. The author let a child ask Confucius to judge a dispute between his friend and himself regarding if the sun was closer to people in the morning or at the noon. The original document was:

Confucius went east, saw two children argued. He asked the point. One child said "I believe that the sun is closer to people in the morning and farther at noon. But he said farther in the morning and closer at noon." Another child said "In the morning the sun is as large as a cover of a wagon , when it's noon, it looks like a size of dish; the bigger the closer isn't it?" The first child said: "The sun is cold in the morning but it is hot like touching hot soup. The hotter the closer isn't it?" Confucius was unable to make a judgment. Both children laughed and said "Who said you were knowledgeable?"

That old question was answered when people understand the deflection of sunshine by the atmosphere.

When the sun is below the horizon, the lights are refracted so that it looks like locating above the horizon and the volume is enlarged by the refraction as well. The density of air is higher each year due to air pollution so that the time of sunrise will show up earlier each year and sunset will delay a little bit more each year.

Besides the refraction, it was the continuous effort from Nicolaus Copernicus (1473-2-19 to 1543-5-24), Galileo Galilei (1564-2-15 to 1642-1-8) to Isaac Newton (1643-1-4 to 1727-3-31) which caused people to abandon the earth centered theory since Claudius Ptolemy (year 90 to168). After that, the question related to above "two children argued about the sun" is fully explained. In case the story was added by other author after Leizi, it still appeared longer than 1600 year ago when Zhang Zhan explained it. Attached picture on page 10 is the evidence.

However, even if someone tried hard to solve the conflict about the sun, no one would know the atmosphere and no one would imagine the ground was like a ball and the earth was circling around the sun while self-spinning.

A good question might not get an answer soon. Nevertheless, good questions and answers are responsible for the accumulation of human knowledge.

Now, there are many questions people do not have answer yet. From the well-known questions like how the crop circles created? Is there an UFO? Is there a ghost? Is there a God? Why is there no natural antiparticle? Why does the speed of light independent from the speed of the source of light? Or, if the gravity force is the combination of the stronger attractive force between different charges and the weaker repulsive force in between same kind of charges? All of these questions belong to the young generation.

A good question like "Two Children argued about the Sun" is hard to find because what it asked was "a conflict people must solve".

Some invention like toilet, sewer and waste water treatment system, electricity, telegraph, telephone, light bulb, movie, radio, refrigerator, TV, computer, internet, smart phone…etc. were all caused by brilliant questions. However, most of them were question of "how", only a few of "why" and none of them was "conflict people must solve".

The most recent conflict people must solve was an experiment designed by Michelson (1852-12-19 to 1931-5-9) in year 1881.

My book started from this conflict people must solve to define time and space. Then I mentioned about other two conflicts people must solve to study with readers.

In the last chapter, I talked about a method I thought about recently which may solve the conflicts.

What I did is to provide a step stone so that it may be easier for readers to find better solutions.

Source Huang
2015-3-15

Chapter 1. Unsolved Conflicts

Due to the experiment is not accurate enough Mr. Michelson redid it with Mr. Morley (1838-1-29 to 1923-2-24) in year 1887 and finished a famous experiment, the Michelson-Morley experiment, MMX).

Physicists repeated MMX at different locations and times and the accuracies increased every time. Combined the results most physicists concluded that they need Lorentz Transformation (LT) to solve the conflict caused by MMX.

After more than 100 years, with support from most scientists, LT finally occupied its position in the physics text books.

Most scientists accepted the hypotheses of "length contraction" and "time dilation" so that they changed the classical idea about time and space before 20th century.

But, what scientists did for the conflict people must solve, MMX, was not as clear as what they did in explaining the conflict of "two children argued about the sun".

1-1. The Unsolved experimental conflict

There were at least two points that MMX was not explained clearly. The first point was that scientists hid a secret. The secret was Ives-Stilwell experiment showed a result opposite to the expectation of Special Relativity (SR). Please refer to the section 3-1 of this book for more detail.

1-2. The Unsolved mathematical conflict

Another point that MMX was not explained clearly was about the mathematical proofs of LT. Einstein tried twice in year 1905 and 1920 and both of them were failed. Please refer to the book "Special Relativity of Roses & Happiness" for more detail. Other proofs were incomplete as well.

1-3. A conflict which is very easy to solve

Actually, the conflict related to MMX that people must solve is very easy to solve. All people need is to compare the vectors representing the velocity of photons and the velocity of the source of light. Please refer to the book "Lorentz Transformation for High School Students".

But, most physicists not only refused to analyze above vectors but also did not check the mathematical proofs of LT to find out wrong procedures. They simply used LT, SR and General Relativity (GR) to solve the conflict related to MMX.

1-4. The Faulty Science of 20th Century

Actually LT, SR and GR are faulty science of 20th century.

First of all, about the names, both of SR and GR are fake "relativity" already. When SR was extended from constant velocity to constant speed on 1905-6-30, in case of circular constant speed motion there is no inversed-SR. People may assume inversed-LT but when they talk about GPS, there is no inverse-SR for circular motion. The extended SR had lost its identity as a classical relativity.

In the real world, there is no inverse-GR and theoretically speaking there is no "relative gravitational strength" to reverse "gravitational strength".

That means SR and GR must comingle the space and time, go beyond classical relativity to play its trick of rotation around the fixed origin point in the four dimension spacetime.

Secondly, by definition, LT is unable to coexist with SR. When the observer of the moving system uses the contracted ruler and dilated clock to measure the relative speed, it will be $(\gamma^2)v$. That means, with SR, there is no more inverse-LT at all.

Addition to it, mathematically speaking, SR is unable to fulfill the operation of function. If the relative velocity of system S'' is 2v to S so that it is v to S', let $\gamma=f(v)$, then, according to SR we have $t''=t/f(2v)$, then due to $t''=t'/f(v)$ and $t'=t/f(v)$ we would have $t''=t/(f(v)^2)$ so that $f(2v)=(f(v))^2$ and it is true only if $v=0$ or $v > c$. That means SR is against to function rules, mathematically.

And, in logic, if S is the stationary system of the universe, then, when we put the rulers of the observers O and O' along the x-axis, we would see the ruler of O is longer than the ruler of O' according to LT. However, if we let the inverse-LT to coexist, we would see two real rulers are longer than each other and that is impossible logically speaking.

No matter judging from the name of relativity, the definition of same relative speed v, the function theory of mathematics, or the logic of real rulers all of LT, SR and GR are fake science.

1-5. Unsolved Conflicts

I will explain in detail at chapter 3 regarding why MMX is still an unsolved conflict to most physicists.

In this book, I will introduce a set of equations named "Distance Transformation" (DT). If Galilean Transformation (GT) is a theoretical version, then, DT is a practical version of GT.

Additionally, I will introduce the "Dynamic Gravitation Formula" established by Tang, Ke Yun. If the gravitation formula created by Newton is useful for stationary stars only, then, the "Dynamic Gravitation Formula" (DGF) is useful for moving stars.

The practical version of GT and the DGF, in the absolute space and time, would be able to support all kinds of requirement for current technologies.

In the stationary absolute space, the absolute time advances with a constant speed and pushes continuous events one by one into the history.

Under this simple and clear spacetime, Chinese culture suggested to focus on the current world and make it peaceful. Within this culture, people did not know how long their soul would survive after totally disappear after they died; might be 7 days or 49 days; but they also hoped that their ancestors and great people in the history would protect them from above forever.

Hindu and Buddhists suggested that people would reborn into the world but if they follow true teachings then their souls might escape the circulation and stay at a paradise in the west.

Catholic, Christians and Moslem suggested that there is one God and hoped their souls might stay with their God in the heaven after they died.

On the road of searching for truth, I will give the time and space a perfect definition then talk about two conflicts people must solve. Before that, let me introduce the twisted spacetime born in the 20th century.

Chapter 2. Democracy and Science

The principle of democracy contains only two key points, be profitable and practical.

After Einstein published his paper on 1905-6-30 about the space and time, claimed that he proved the Lorentz Transformation (LT) mathematically; the science was heading to democratization. Why?

2-1. Democratic Science - Timing & Location

The hypothesis of "length contraction" had pended for more than 10 years in Europe and people still did not know if it would solve the conflict created by MMX so that when people heard someone already proved the LT mathematically, most likely people would try to design an experiment to verify it.

2-2. Democratic Science - the Event Itself

Some scholars did question about both proofs of LT provided by Einstein, but, the results of experiments were more important than the mathematical proofs so that both of LT and SR were successfully attracted physicists to study them in depth.

2-3. Democratic Science - the Factor of Support

Einstein was able to get a lot of supports. In year 1907, one of his teachers already created the Minkowski Space to explain SR geometrically. After Einstein published his GR formally in year 1916, the first non-trivial solution of the GR equation was found by Karl Schwazchild. Then the theory of Black Holds was established later on. Even Einstein's mistake of adding the cosmological constant was able to be corrected due to the theory of Big Bang.

2-4. Democratic Science - Factor of Resources

In the factor of resources, the quick expansion of science from atom, nucleus, particles, computers and websites all helped people to link more and more observations or experiments to GR and SR.

Went through the golden era of GR, from year 1960 to 1975, even if the GR and quantum theory were not compatible to each other, even if there was no experiment to verify "length contraction", most physicists still decided to accept the "length contraction" and "time dilation" as proved physical fact.

The mixed space and time was finally created in the 20th century and the "Democratic Science" was established in the 20th century as well.

2-5. Science

The principles of science has only two main points which are matching fact and be reasonable. When there is no fact to match all science's concern will be "reasonable" only. Then, are LT and SR reasonable?

Let me explain logic and physics briefly and say something about the phenomena about the power of life and rushing for the first, then I will select two facts to show you that both of LT and SR are not reasonable.

2-6. Logic

Mathematics is the best material in teaching logic. Reasonable is logically matching the fact. Logic is the tool to check if something is reasonable or not.

Logic is to find the main factor when people choose.

However, most people do not use logic. Most people do their job robotically. When face a choice more than half of people are "passive"; you know, in general, when a person is forced to choose there are only a few poor opportunities.

There is an old Chinese saying that the wise move before the chance, the smart change upon the chance, the vulgar follow after the change and the stupid regret upon every missed chance.

Since following the change already delayed, it is to select from a few second choices; then, most likely a decision of the vulgar would be regretful, isn't it?

In my opinion, the election of leaders may miss chance, the vote of laws will most likely miss chance and to decide a scientific law by voting will definitely miss the chance of catching fact.

2-7. Physics

There are two major differences between mathematics and physics: at the maximum and at the minimum.

The total amount of objects would be limited and there is no real things come with zero volume but in mathematics there is an idea of infinite like the number of all integers and there are something come with zero volume like a point, a line and a plane.

However, since science is the knowledge come with formula, physics is part of science so that physics is linked to mathematics automatically.

2-8. The Power of Life

Living creatures have power to move against to physical laws.

Physicists are part of living creatures and they can act against to their own wills as well, sometimes, if the situation is beyond their control.

2-9. Rush for the First

Since most physicists are part of the vulgar, with common talents, they have to follow the change so that LT, even not proved, is very hot and something built on top of it, like SR and GR are getting more and more popular.

It is like building a skyscraper on top of a piece of land before studying the structure of the ground, all because the builder wants to chase the expected opportunity in the market.

Schools and governments all rush for being the first organization which discovers or verifies some new laws in fundamental physics.

Chapter 3. Assumed Spacetime

In this chapter I will provide two evidences to show you why the science in 20th century was a democratic science.

Let us think about the foundation of science first. Physics is the foundation of science because spirit is beyond science. Then, what is the foundation of physics? Since science depends on record and record must have location and time, I will say the foundation of physics is also a solid common understanding of the space and time among physicists.

There are three new famous theories of physics in the 20th century. Besides the uncertainty principle, there were assumed hypotheses related to the space and time; the assumed "length contraction" and "time dilation". All of them are accepted by text books and have been taught in schools.

But, in an experiment related to SR, some physicists hid a fact and in LT, mathematically speaking, it actually support :time speeding"! Let me tell you some more details.

3-1. Ives-Stilwell experiment (1938)

The result of this experiment was against to the expectation of SR in the direction of change. The Doppler effect expected the average of wavelengths measured by observing a source of light moving at constant velocity v relative to the observer, one when leaving and one when approaching, will remain the same as it is at rest under any velocity v.

The experiment verified that the average would decrease if v becomes faster. That means, the Doppler effect needs some modification. However, SR expected the average wavelength would increase if v becomes faster.

To handle this problem, most physicists decided to focus on the amount of change and ignore or hide the direction of the change.

3-2. The Truth of LT (1889/1892)

According to the book "Lorentz Transformation for High School Students" LT is so simple that:

when v=0, it is (t', x', y', z')=(t, x, y, z) and
when v>0, it is (t', x', y', z') = (γt, -γvt, y, z).

Chapter 4: the Truth of Space and Time

GR suggested that the speed of time is slower in a stronger gravitational field.

Einstein combined the classical space and time into four dimensional spacetime via the force field; the force field includes gravitational force, kinetic force and all non-gravitational force beyond kinetic force, and, Einstein simplified all forces other than kinetic force be considered the same by his "equivalence principle". Under that arrangement, all objects would follow the shortest distance within the twisted spacetime.

GR suggested that the spacetime tells matters how to move and matters tell spacetime how to bend.

What contemporary scholars believe is that Einstein's GR will reduce to SR when the gravitational field is very weak and SR will reduce to the classic Newton's physics when the relative speed is very small compared with the speed of light.

In this chapter, I will explain the truth of space and time in detail with respects of "length contraction",. "moving time dilation" and "compressing time dilation" .

4-1. Length Contraction

Even we accept the hypothesis of length contraction, the formula is not so simple as described in LT.

First of all, the spatial equation in Galilean Transformation (GT) is x'=x-vt' mathematically speaking. However, t'=t in GT so that the equation of x'=x-vt in GT is also true within assumption of GT, which is assumed there are observers everywhere in S and S'.

That assumption is gone in LT, hence, x'=x-vt is no longer true in the environment of LT, in which only two observers are allowed. When Mr. Lorentz applied his hypothesis of length contraction, he should not use x'=x-vt. The correct one to use is x'=x-vt' and the way to apply it will be very complicated.

Secondly, if both of the starting event and ending event are happened in the S' then there is no way to apply the length contraction principle because both points in S' will contract under the same way of the rulers used in S' so that we cannot apply the Lorentz factor to the measurement in S' unless the observer in S' mark the event location in the system S and measure the marked two points in S.

Physicists do not have common understanding about the above two issues yet. They should think about the issues and provide a clear definition of LT for people.

4-2. The Monster in the 3-dimension Space

Now, let's imagine what kind of monsters we will be under LT. If a space shuttle was running at 0.867c then the effect of length contraction would be larger than 50%.

That meant, if the pilot turned his head to talk to the vice-pilot, then his face would change from a flat circle to a thin oval. And when he finished talking and turned his head to the front, his face would change back to a flat circle again.

Do you think our skulls can handle it?

4-3. Moving and Compressing Time Dilations

The GPS explanation provided by SR and GR was based on the action Einstein took in 1905, he let SR be true when v was a constant SPEED. That expansion from LT allowed SR to apply in the situation of circling motion.

However Einstein did not think deep enough regarding if the speed of time would change when the speed of clock changed.

The speed of clocks might change due to different environments like different gravitational potentials. But some clocks would run faster in stronger field and some clocks would run slower in stronger field so that how could we know which one was matching the nature's way of the time change if the speed of time changed?

4-4. There are two observers in LT

Normally a text book would let observers in LT stay at their origin points and would name the observers as O and O' for the system S and S' respectively. If we allowed observers in S and S' be available at every location then the event time could be recorded the same by the observers at the event location so that the t'=t in GT would make sense.

Base on that simple distance factor, let's start to define time.

4-5. An Event Time-point

To understand why the speed of time could be recorded differently by two observers, we must understand what is an event time-point first.

I adopted the idea of a frozen universe in a Korean drama series named “My Love from another Star” to show “an event time-point” which is the time an event happens.

Time is always moving and if we pick up another frozen universe after the previous one, there will be a section of time in between two event time-points.

Base on the idea of frozen universes, time is moving from one frozen universe to another frozen universe in a way that there are unlimited frozen universes in between any two different frozen universes. If we consider heart beats as events then the event times can be considered as points of integers on the axis of time. An axis of time is quite the same as an axis of real numbers.

4-6. Time Axis

If we select a point on the time axis to represent now, then each event happened before can find one and only one corresponding point to represent its event time-point after we assign one point for one, any one, event happened before now.

The reason for different observers to record different event times for same event is very complicated, but, there are at least two main factors. One is the distance away from the event and the other one is the clocks are not exactly synchronized.

4-7. Tow imaginary Event Time-points

In this section I started two imaginary events to explain why the speed of time is independent from the speed of clocks.

Based on the setup of LT, I let a lightbulb stayed at point A by a road closed to O and O’ and assumed the velocity of O and O’ were v and 2v relative to the earth respectively.

The event E1 was the lightbulb being turned on at time t1 and the event E2 was the lightbulb was turned off at time t2.

Since the earth was self-spinning, the location of A in the universe should be different at time t1 and t2.

I assumed the locations of O,O' and A in the frozen universe at time t1 were O1, O'1 and A1while the locations in the frozen universe at t2 were O2, O'2 and A2 respectively.

4-8. An Absolute stationary Point

In the next step, I assumed that people could see photons even if the photons did not enter their eyes, or let me asked people to image it, then we would see two spheres of photon skin raped a shell of photons. The thickness of that shell was about (t2-t1)c and the center of the big sphere was A1 while the center of the small sphere was A2 as shown on the diagram.

Assumed that the large sphere reached O and O' at time t1o and t1o' and the small sphere reached O and O' at time t2o and t2o', that meant the time between events E1 and E2 were recorded by O and O' as (t2o-t1o) and (t2o'-t1o') respectively.

If (t2o-t1o) was different from (t2o'-t1o') it was because the distance between A and observers were different or two clocks were not synchronized. The time period between two frozen universes were all the same to any two observers in the universe is very obvious.

If t2 was very close to t1 then the shell could be very thin. If t2=t1, then the shell would be just a layer of skin which was expanding in the universe.

In that case, A1 was a stationary point in the universe while the radius of the photon sphere was expanding at the speed of light.

4-9. The Absolute Speed of Time

As a matter of fact, the length of the path that any photon went through in between two frozen universes were always the same, it was (t2-t1)c.

You may say the speed of light in water is slower than c, in that case, you should say the velocity of light is slower in water while the speed of light remains the same in water; because the path of the light is zigzag in the water.

We may define the speed of time is the speed of light.

Then, how do we define the speed of light? We may select a ray with a fix wavelength then count the number of the peaks received by a device to measure the speed of time.

For example, if we use green light to make a computerized watch with a built-in source of green light and a receiver so that when the counting number reaches 1877934, thc time period is about 1 three-hundred-billionth of second, I named it one photond.

The speed of light will be 1 meter/photond.

I hope the source of green light in the device will not change the wavelength of the light it emits, when we move it from hillside to hilltop or from equator to north pole. If my hope is true, then we will have a watch to measure the speed of the absolute time.

If we can use a higher frequency of EM-wave as the source of light then we can measure the speed of time more accurately.

Chapter 5: Cai, Zhi-Zhong

I introduced Cai, Zhi-Zhong because he created a formula for the speed of absolute time and published it in year 2010.

His formula for measuring the absolute time is "to a source of light, the time of an object is equal to (the number of observed wave peaks x wavelength)/the speed of light)

He mentioned about if the speed of an object is faster than the speed of light then that object will not receive any wave peak so that there will be no time to that object.

His answer to that problem of his formula is that, all matter of non-zero mass will not move faster than light.

5-1. The Twin Paradox

In this section, I explained how to treat the twin paradox by his formula.

5-2. The Mistake made by Einstein

According to Cai, Zhi-Zhong, Einstein forgot to check the clock at the station in the front when Einstein said the clock at the station behind him would run slower if the train went faster and if the train ran at the speed of light, that clock would look like stop running.

5-3. What is a photon?

According to Mr. Cai, people still didn't understand photons.

However, he assumed that photons was the common language between intelligent living creatures of the universe.

5-4. U-second

Mr. Cai said we might define the speed of light as 1 unit and took the chance to define all units by using "length" and "time" only. That meant, the G in the formula of GM=(V^2)R must be absorbed by either the speed V or the radius R.

Mr. Cai suggested that people might reach the goal by two steps, first step was to define 1 U-second = ((1000G)^(1/2)) second. Then defined 1 U-kilometer=1156188834 kilometer and after that we would have the speed of light as 1 U-kilometer/U-second.

5-5. Go Mr. Cai

I mentioned about Mr. Cai did not talk about how electric charges appear in his formulas and both of his formula and Einstein's formula of E=mc^2 were missing the heat energy.

Chapter 6: Stephen Hawking

I introduced his book, A Brief History of Time, a little bit.

6-1. How absolute space & time disappeared

Mr. Hawking described that portion of history in the chapter 2 of that book and I summarized it.

6-2. The Uncertainty Principle

I also summarized the chapter 4 of that book.

6-3. No Boundary Condition

I also summarized the chapter 8 of that book.

6-4. Quantum Emission from Black Holes

I wondered if GR will change to "GR without LT" after LT is abandoned by people.

6-5. Two missed Chances

I mentioned about two chances that Mr. Hawking missed in the chapter 2 of that book, A Brief History of Time.

The first one was between figure 2.2 and 2.3 where he could find a stationary point in the universe.

The second one is between figure 2.7 and 2.8 where he could apply the speed of gravity to Newton's gravitational equation and reach the same solid improvement done by Tang Ke-Yun in year 2012.

Chapter 7: Tang Ke-Yun

Tang Ke-Yun verified that the speed of gravitational force is the same as the speed of light in year 2011 and extended Newton's gravitational equation from stationary environment to the real universe in year 2012.

7-1. Hubble's Law

People still don't understand what Hubble's Law will affect the universe. I mentioned about four problems people must find solution to keep our earth livable and the study of the following four topics would help people to solve the four problems.

7-2. Anti-matters

7-3. Photons

7-4. Muon Decay

7-5. UFO

Chapter 8: Distance Transformation

The Distance Transformation (DT) is based on a simple fact that the recorded event time will never come before the actual event time. I said the DT was the practical version of GT, with two observers only. I believe that the DT can replace LT.

8-1. Software and Fact

In this section I talked about four kinds of change in the real world that are hard to handle when updating the software to match the changes. I also talked about a hidden trouble created by computer which is "all city residents were heavily relying on computer to survive in the 21st century".

8-2. Temporary Work-Flow

People will need temporary work-flow if the software can be updated. If an update is impossible, then, people must build a new software.

8-3. Harmonic Physical World

The LT, SR and GR have created a temporary work-flow for physics study. The influence of that temporary work-flow is very small or tiny because the total numbers of physicists is just a very tiny portion of human beings.

I hope people will find out the reason why an atomic clock will run slower in a stronger gravitational field quick enough. After that, people will be able to bring the absolute space and time back to the real world.

Chapter 9: Two Conflicts must be solved

The scientific knowledge increased a lot after the 1760 Industrial Revolution. The democratic government started from America in year 1776 but it was unable to spread all over the world until the end of World War II.

In our history, a tyrant would not last long but an everlasting democratic government is not only inefficient but also late or never responding to troubles.

9-1. The vulgar follow the change

There is an old saying in China states: "The wise move before a chance appear, the smart change when a chance appear, the vulgar follow the change made by the smart and the stupid regret for the missed chances they can see."

Basically, a democratic government is controlled by the vulgar. When the vulgar follow the change made by the smart, the problem is worse than it was at the time when the smart made the change. That means, the vulgar are unable to solve a problem properly. So, here is one conflict must be solved:

The vulgar cannot hold the power but do not solve problems, right?

9-2. Statistics

I talked about teachers have adopted statistics to all possible knowledge to make them part of science, but, there are still quite a few knowledge left beyond the territory of science.

9-3. So-called Knowledge

I defined the knowledge just like what I did in the book "APA, a Dialog of Spacetime"

9-4. Good Choices

I talked about people use computer to help them make quick decisions.

Even that method can apply to science and business only, due to the fact that people tend to claim that their main goal of life is be a successful merchant in this day, I think, in the 21st century, a computerized good choice is indeed a good choice so long as the selected samples are a kind of objective.

Today, almost everybody wants to be a successful merchant.

9-5. Profits

I talked about profits a little bit.

9-6. Love, Justice and Offspring

In this section I mentioned about the change of the goal of life in the last 100 years.

While the accomplishment of some achievements, virtual samples or valuable books shrunk to simply a successful business, the purpose of life has also shrunk from care of love, justice and offspring to simply a comfortable living.

In the 19th century, all people honored was a life with true love or strong justice. As of today, in the 21st century, there is no change to the meaning of the words love and justice, what missing now is the brave to achieve them.

The goal of the vulgar in the 19th century was to establish a home and then a business. Now a day, to establish a home is not necessary so that establish a business is such a simple goal that all people need now is knowledge of science. Or, to make it even easier, all people need now is the skill of handling a cell phone efficiently.

9-7. Comfortable Living

I talked about it was not easy to establish a business, either a secured job or the owner of a long lasting business. That meant, it was not easy to maintain a comfortable living as of yesterday.

9-8. Be Wise, Kind and Brave

In this section I talked about people loved the story about some wise, kind or brave guys, so long as the story teller made it interesting. In the virtual world created by computer games people could make themselves the main role of the story they liked the most.

To be wise, kind or brave is to reach truth, perfectness and beauty respectively. Since things with value only occupied a small area of truth, as a business owner or holder of a secured job, the person loses most truth, ignored perfectness and afraid of being brave.

9-9. Practical/Useful Events

People dreamed about being a brave person, taking care of love or justice; but in the real world they were afraid of being brave.

Because, a merchant does not need to be brave due to money can solve almost all problems in the 21st century.

That was another conflict people must solve. I named it a modern conflict.

I think the information people should hand down must include at least the following two kinds of history. One is the detail information about a wonderful art work and the other one is the detail of a piece of great history, an event a great person performed. I named those two kinds of information as practical events.

The effect of teaching or providing details of practical events may appear too slowly but I believe those actions could solve the modern conflict in the long run.

Chapter 10. Seattle-Taiwanese Entrepreneurs-Promoting Association

A proposal of Seattle-Taiwanese Entrepreneurs-Promoting Association (STEPA)

Seattle-Taiwanese Entrepreneurs-Promoting Association is a group to be organized soon. Its English name is STEPA.

In my mind, the members of STEPA are Taiwanese who have stable economic support either retired or a business owner in Seattle area. STEPA members do not pay any fee and there is no office for STEPA. The chief board member will decide how long is that position and the list of all members as well as projects reports are all in a free website to be decided.

The purpose of STEPA is to work together for providing jobs.

That means, since being established, members of STEPA like to help establishing people.

The way STEPA works is to create all kinds of special business groups, like SEAA in 10-1, to find prospective established business owners who want to start a special business based on the wage system of clean & abled management and the principle of reinvestment.

Wage system: clean & abled management

The hourly wage and the benefits of a frontline worker is the same as average from same kind of jobs in the local area.

The lead-worker is a frontline worker who is also responsible for on-job training and handling emergency conditions like absent without notice and time sensitive issues so that the treatment is 105% of the highest treatment of frontline workers under the lead.

All other managers are paid average of wage and benefits of all workers directly report to the manager.

Profit distribution: no more than 15%

In the first 5 years, no more than 5% of profit can be distributed to stock holders; it will be no more than 10% of profit from the 6th year to the 10th year, then, no more than 15% after that. The rest of profit should be used to improve the business or open new branches.

10-1. Seattle virtuous-Events and wonderful-Arts Association (SEAA)

Select an owner of Chinese newspaper in Seattle area like Asia Today, Seattle Chinese Post, Chinese Seattle News (Washington Chinese post, Seattle Chinese Journal) and Seattle Chinese Times etc. or a person with leadership be the chief board member of SEAA and I will be the contact person. The purpose of SEAA is to create a business named Great virtuous-Events and Great wonderful-Arts Weekly Inc. (GeGaWI) to publish a weekly magazine named GeGa Weekly to report the practical events as defined in the section 9-9 for two kinds of information only. There are three stages:

Stage 1: I will look for the starting members, including the chief board member, then the chief board member registers the foundation with 52% of the total investment and other founding members contribute the rest 48%.

Stage 2: Find an established Chinese newspaper or magazine like Taiwan News, Epoch News or Commonwealth Magazine etc. to create GeGaWI with two to three sponsors like stated in details on page 115 and the following pages.

Stage 3: Sold GeGaWI to Google or other international big company so that GeGa Weekly will belong to the new GeWeekly or XeWeekly to make itself a global magazine.

List of members: Name, phone #, email address

Page 131, readers may organize some other groups to solve the pending conflicts that people must solve, as soon as possible.

Printed in the United States
By Bookmasters